In the firing line

war and children's rights

AMNESTY
INTERNATIONAL
UNITED KINGDOM

In the firing line: War and children's rights

Cover photograph: Displaced child, Liberia 1997
© Jenny Matthews

Printed by Ennisfield Print and Design
January 1999

ISBN 1873328346
AIUK Product Ref PB170

Contents

Introduction

For too long, we have given ground to spurious claims that the involvement of children in armed conflict is regrettable but inevitable. It is not. Children are regularly caught up in conflict because of conscious and deliberate decisions made by adults.

Graça Machel, The impact of armed conflict on children. Report to the United Nations General Assembly, 26 August 1996.

Children have the right to grow up without being bombed from their homes or beaten by soldiers. Boys and girls have the right not to be raped by armed fighters. They have the right not to be killed or kidnapped or press-ganged into armies. They have the right not to be murdered because of their poverty, or their race or religion, or because of their parents. They have the right to grow up free from fear and persecution, free to have and express their own opinions and beliefs.

As the new millennium dawns, children across the globe have their rights violated on an epic scale. In the last decade, millions of children have been killed, maimed and wounded in wars and armed conflicts, big and small. Those that survive carry lifelong physical and psychological scars which will blight whole societies for generations.

In the 10 years since the Convention on the Rights of the Child was adopted by the United Nations on 20 November 1989, 191 countries have ratified it – every country in the world except the USA and Somalia. Governments are bound by international law to protect children's rights. The most widely supported of all international treaties, the Convention offers a message of hope for future protection of children's rights. But this hope will only be translated into a reality for the millions of children caught up in the world's wars if it is accompanied by a change in public, political and military attitudes.

The involvement of children in warfare – as participants and as targets – should be treated with the same abhorrence currently reserved

Children play in war-devastated Lobito, Angola, 1997.

© Jenny Matthews

for chemical and biological weapons, which are banned from use because of their inherent cruelty and undiscriminating impact.

Humanitarian principles have been used to codify the conduct of war since the adoption of the initial Geneva Convention in 1864, which allowed wounded soldiers to be seen as victims in need of treatment and not as legitimate targets. These twin principles of humanitarian law – that you can distinguish between legitimate and illegitimate targets in war and that certain cruel behaviour is itself illegitimate – have been used ever since to define the 'proper' conduct of warfare.

These principles need to be applied explicitly to include children. It is no accident when the overwhelming majority of casualties in warfare are civilians – and most of them children. It is no accident when indiscriminate weapons, and military tactics which involve recruiting child soldiers or terrorising civilians, are used. Someone chooses to use those weapons, to recruit children, to force civilian populations from their homes and land. When children fleeing conflict are refused sanctuary in other countries, it is because someone has decided to deny them shelter.

Amnesty International believes the plague of violations against children is not inevitable: they are the result of human decisions and can be stopped. This book seeks to demonstrate the scale and scope of children's involvement in armed conflicts today. It is by no means a comprehensive account of the horrors inflicted on children today: but it gives a shocking glimpse of the scale of the problem.

The book includes contributions from several expert authors, drawing on Amnesty International and other sources. In *War against childhood*, Maggie Black outlines how human rights violations in the late 1990s are increasingly associated with war or internal armed conflict. As patterns of conflict have changed, so have the patterns of human rights violations. Women and children are likely to be not only the primary casualties but the actual targets of modern conflict, with mass refugee flows, growing numbers of imploding states, and protracted internal armed conflict – and with rape and torture used as weapons of war, and children forcibly recruited as soldiers. On the positive side, there has been progress towards a 'child rights culture', and children's rights do have a special place in international law.

In *Casualties of conflict*, Robert Beasley highlights the many ways that wars hurt children, drawing on cases from Rwanda, Algeria, Northern Uganda, Sudan, Yugoslavia, Sierra Leone, Colombia, Turkey, South Asia. These show the devastating psychological trauma suffered by children, the deadly menace of landmines, and other kinds of war against children, such as the 'social cleansing' of street children in Brazil, Colombia and Guatemala.

Rachel Brett, in *Child soldiers: Armed and dangerous*, examines how two modern developments have contributed to the growing use of children as soldiers: the development of lightweight automatic weapons which can make a 10-year-old child an effective weapon of destruction, and the shift in the nature of war with battles carried out within civilian populations rather than as pitched battles between state armed forces. At least 300,000 youngsters under 18 are engaged in active combat. *War, Child Soldiers, and UK arms*, in map and information form from (*next page and inside back cover*) shows graphically the pattern of conflict in the world today — and notes the destinations of some UK licensed arms exports.

The massive explosion in child refugees is highlighted in *Forced to flee: Refugee children* by Simon Russell. More than half of any refugee population will be children, which means there are around 14 million children who are refugees or internally 'displaced persons'. Children face particular problems when fleeing conflict or persecution, especially when they are unaccompanied. The chapter outlines the rights of refugee children, and focuses on the responsibilities – and responses – of the international community.

In *War and children's rights*, Dan Seymour examines the role of the comprehensive UN Convention on the Rights of the Child and international moves to raise the minimum age for recruitment of children as soldiers to 18. The protection of children should be a priority in time of armed conflict, both because of their extreme vulnerability, and because of their crucial role in any future peace and post-conflict reconstruction. They must also be recognised as potential actors in their own right. The chapter highlights the need to tackle the issue of impunity – and to make recruiting child soldiers a war crime.

Arms – and human rights casualties

The UN Children's Fund and UNHCR have estimated that there were over 200,000 child soldiers in armed conflicts in 25 countries and it has been reported by the Office of the UN Special Representative for Children in Armed Conflict that in the past decade alone, about 2 million children have been killed in armed conflict. In addition, some 44 countries recruit children under the age of 18 to serve in national armies. Many of these countries have ongoing internal conflicts. Amnesty International believes that the total number of youngsters under 18 engaged in active combat is at least 300,000.

Britain has a special responsibility to ensure that its military, security, police exports do not contribute to the violation of children's human rights as it has become the world's second largest supplier of defence equipment and British companies own some of the world's largest small arms manufacturers such as Heckler & Koch and Smith & Wesson.

> '...A catalogue entry by the gun maker Smith & Wesson, for example, shows a young child who appears to be about 12 aiming a handgun with his father beside him: "Seems like only yesterday that your father brought you here for the first time" the ad says. "Those sure were the good times – just you, dad and his Smith & Wesson..."'
>
> International Herald Tribune. March 30, 1998.

UK exports fuelling conflicts?

In the absence of comprehensive reports from the UK government on small arms transfers, one approach is to compare the countries to which the United Kingdom granted export licences for small arms, with countries suffering from conflicts. The Dutch organisation PIOOM publish a map *(see back cover)* identifying the number and intensity of conflicts occurring worldwide in 1996/7. PIOOM is the Interdisciplinary Research Program on Root Causes of Human Rights Violations, at the Centre for the Study of Social Conflicts, Leiden University, the Netherlands. Much of its current work has been devoted to establishing an early warning system to prevent genocide.

PIOOM distinguishes five levels of conflict, namely: peacefulness; political tension (below 25 political killings); violent political conflict [VPC] (fewer than 100 fatalities in one year); low-intensity conflict [LIC]

Countries receiving UK ML1* category small arms in 1995 / Conflict zones			
Region	Number of countries receiving ML1 category small arms	Number of countries identified as 'conflict zones'	% of countries supplied with UK ML1 small arms that are 'conflict zones'
Africa	16	11	69
Asia	13	9	69
Latin America & Caribbean	17	7	41
Middle East	12	4	33

*The Export of Goods (Control) Order code ML1 denotes: Small arms, machine guns and accessories.

(between 100 and 1000 fatalities); and high intensity conflict [HIC] (more than 1,000 fatalities).

The table above compares the number of countries that received ML1 category export licences from the United Kingdom in 1995, and the number of countries within the regions of Africa, Asia, Latin America and the Caribbean, and the Middle East defined by PIOOM as having either High Intensity Conflicts, Low Intensity Conflicts, or Violent Political Conflicts.

It can be seen in Africa and Asia that 69 per cent of the countries receiving small arms from the United Kingdom were defined by PIOOM as conflict zones. It is highly likely that many of the victims of these small arms in these countries were children.

The full data for exports from the United Kingdom since the introduction of the UK government's ethical foreign policy were not available by early 1999. However, from data provided for a partial list of countries to Members of Parliament (written Parliamentary Answer to Menzies Campbell MP, 10 June 1998), it is possible to see that the government has continued to grant export licences to countries that are currently suffering internal conflicts.

Between 1 May 1997 and 10 May 1998, ML1 licences were granted to the following countries: Bahrain, Colombia, India, Indonesia, Jordan, Kenya, Mexico, Morocco, Pakistan, Saudi Arabia, Sri Lanka, Syria, Turkey, Uganda, Yemen, Zambia, Zimbabwe.

War against childhood

Maggie Black

'What's the point of the war? Why, oh, why can't people live peacefully together? Why all this destruction? Why are millions spent on the war each day, while not a penny is available for medical science, artists or the poor? Why do people have to starve when mountains of food are rotting away? Oh, why are people so crazy? I don't believe the war is simply the work of politicians and capitalists. The common man is every bit as guilty. There's a destructive urge in people, the urge to rage, murder and kill.'

The most famous testimony from a child caught in the coils of conflict is that of 15-year-old Anne Frank. She wrote these words in her diary a few months before she was herded onto a train bound for a Nazi concentration camp, and death. Her story has resonated down the years, exemplifying the ultimate abuse of childhood and destruction of young promise that armed persecution can represent. War itself did not bring about her death; but war was the context for the gross violations of human rights which caused Anne Frank to perish.

Today, millions of young people witness the horrors of conflict and organised violence. Here is an account by a 14-year-old Ugandan girl of her abduction by armed aggressors in February 1997: 'I had gone to the garden at around eight in the morning. Suddenly, I was surrounded by rebels. They started beating me terribly. They wanted me to walk them to my home but I was refusing. Finally we went there and collected my clothes. There, they killed my mother. They made me go, leaving behind my little brother and two little sisters. I was resisting. Then they started beating me until I became unconscious. Life was leaving me but I was thinking of the children.' This is one of many testimonies to appalling acts of brutality to children recorded in a 1997 Amnesty International report on the Lord's Resistance Army (LRA) in northern Uganda.[2]

Child at home, Shatila refugee camp, Beirut, 1998.

© Carlos Reyes-Manzo

In the past five years, the LRA's violations against children's rights have been on an unprecedented scale in today's epidemic of internal strife. Up to 8,000 young boys and girls have been kidnapped to serve as fighters, camp workers, and sexual slaves for rebel commanders.[3] But if the scale is unusual, the nature of these atrocities is becoming painfully commonplace. 'Where there are any little girls, they should be raped', was an instruction radioed by a Liberian warlord to his troops, intercepted by West African peacekeeping forces in 1993.[4] Through the 1990s, similar reports of utter disregard for child rights in places of turmoil have proliferated. The most conspicuous armed conflicts of the decade – in Somalia, Rwanda, Bosnia, Afghanistan, Chechnya, Kosovo – have been characterised by atrocity, and the abandonment of any 'rules of war', starting with abandonment of respect for any distinction between combatants and civilians, or the innocence of children.

Graça Machel's 1996 UN study into the impact of armed conflict on children underlined the changing pattern of warfare in the post-Cold War world:

'More and more of the world is being sucked into a desolate moral vacuum. This is a space devoid of the most basic human values, a space in which children are slaughtered, raped and maimed; a space in which children are exploited as soldiers; and a space in which children are starved and exposed to extreme brutality.'... 'Millions of children are caught up in conflicts in which they are not merely bystanders, but targets.'

In the previous 10 years, Machel estimated, around 2 million children had been killed in armed conflict, three times as many seriously injured or permanently disabled, and countless others forced to witness or take part in horrifying acts of violence.[5]

Reports of acts of violent aggression against children and young people have become routine, even in countries which are not at war in the conventional sense, but where political, economic or social pressure has led to organised violence by groups within society, or by state security forces. In Brazil, Colombia and Guatemala, extra-judicial killing of street children by police forces or hired guns is not

---

[2] Amnesty International, Uganda: *'Breaking God's commands': the destruction of childhood by the Lord's Resistance Army*. September 1997.
[3] Carol Bellamy, Executive Director, UNICEF, CF/DOC/PR/1997/27. Statement 3 July 1997.
[4] Mark Huband, in *The Guardian*, 21 May 1993.

uncommon.[6] In Sri Lanka, children under 17 are among the thousands of people reported as 'disappeared' after detention by security forces and armed groups.[7] In Turkey, children as young as 12 have been tortured in police custody on suspicion of minor offences.[8] In Venezuela, Amnesty International has reported cases of children being arbitrarily detained by the security forces, physically ill-treated, and kept in appalling conditions.[9]

Facts - children and conflict

In the last decade:
• more than 1.5 million children under 18 have been killed;
• at least 10 million children have witnessed acts of war or brutality;
• more than 4 million children have been disabled or maimed;
• more than 12 million children have lost their homes;
• more than 5 million children have been forced to live in camps;
• more than 1 million children are separated from their families;
• at least 300,000 children have been recruited into armed activity;
• 1 million people have been killed by land-mines, many of them children.

Sources: *Children at War*, Save the Children Fund, 1998; Amnesty International

The end of the 20th century has seen a mounting record of agonising abuse of children's rights – a record which ought to have declined in the years since Anne Frank lost her life in the largest and most systematic genocide of all time. At the heart of this crisis in human rights affecting the most vulnerable and dependent members of the human race is the state of upheaval in today's world, and the changing role of conflict and episodic mass violence within it.

---

[5] United Nations, *The Impact of Armed Conflict on Children*, Report of the Expert of the Secretary-General, Ms Graça Machel, submitted pursuant to General Assembly Resolution 48/157, A/51/306, 26 August 1996.
[6] Amnesty International, *Guatemala: State of impunity*, April 1997, and other AI reports.
[7] Amnesty International, *South Asia: Action for Children*, April 1998.
[8] Report of the UN Working Group on Enforced and Involuntary Disappearances, figures for 1994; cited in *Turkey, Children at risk of torture, death in custody, and disappearance*, Amnesty International, November 1996.
[9] Amnesty International, *Venezuela, The silent cry: gross human rights violations against children*, October 1997.

Conflict in flux

'In the years since the end of the cold war, humankind has leap-frogged ahead and stumbled backwards simultaneously. New possibilities for co-operation, community and well-being have opened. At the same time we have witnessed the proliferation of conflicts, an upsurge of intolerance and hatred, and callous abandonment of the most elemental notions of human rights and human dignity.'

James P Grant, Executive Director of UNICEF, at the World Conference on Human Rights, 1993.

At the beginning of the century, approximately 90 per cent of war casualties were military. During the Second World War, civilians accounted for around half of all deaths including the victims of bombing raids and death camps. Today, around three-quarters of war deaths are among civilians. If refugees, the internally displaced and the wounded are added to the toll of human damage, the proportion of civilian casualties rises to 90 per cent.[10] Children constitute a high proportion of any civilian population. In many of the poorer developing countries – the setting for most of today's wars – children under 18 constitute nearly half the population. Thus over 40 per cent of the victims of today's conflicts are typically children and young people.[11]

The invasion of conflict into civilian lives – into their streets, shopping malls, market places, fields and farmyards, even into their homes – is a product of the changing nature of conflict. War as an act of national aggrandisement is now relatively rare. Today, almost all conflicts are within states, rather than between states. The predominant pattern is of armed insurgency opposing armed state authorities. In protracted struggles, the failure of any party to gain the definitive upper hand spawns a splintering process in which armed groups proliferate and their political intentions become obscure. Where modern institutions are flimsy, the effect is to destroy progressively the structures of government and society, creating a downward spiral of violent lawlessness. This pattern is typical of Sierra Leone, Somalia, and southern Sudan; it has also occurred in the

---

[10] Christa Ahlstrom, *Casualties of Conflict*, Uppsala University, Sweden, Department of Peace and Conflict Research, 1991.
[11] UNICEF UK committee, *Children in conflict: a child rights emergency*, Maggie Black, February 1998.

the new republics of the former Soviet Union, Afghanistan, and in parts of many other countries.

Genocide may become an implicit or even explicit aim in some modern conflicts, whatever the initial motivation of the protagonists – political, or territorial, or economic control over an area and its resources. Where ethnicity is an important component of existing power structures, or of a challenge to them – as in Rwanda, Congo, Kosovo, Burma, Mexico, Sudan, and many other conflicts – 'the ethnic other' becomes the target. Whether the 'enemy' carries weapons, is young or old, male or female, becomes irrelevant. All members of the opposing group, not soldiers alone, are in the line of fire. Young people, as the up-coming generation, may even be targeted to reduce the numbers of the future 'enemy'.

Abandoning rules of war – whether traditional codes of warrior conduct, or more recent codes enshrined in international conventions – causes social havoc. People no longer know what to expect or whom to trust. Insecurity is compounded by the lack of effective command structures within loosely-knit armed groups, and of the military discipline of conventional armies. Human rights can be systematically violated since there is no authority willing or able to call them to account.[12] In such an environment, atrocity and counter-atrocity flourish.

Children under 18 become recruited routinely into fighting forces: about 300,000 are estimated to be currently taking part in hostilities around the world.[13] Others may witness, or be made to perpetrate, acts of atrocity. Their vulnerability and susceptibility may be exploited to turn them into instruments of terror – as happens in Northern Uganda. Some rescued children are so disturbed they have come to enjoy torturing. Holding a gun, firing it, and seeing a person drop down has become the only reality they know.[14] Such children bear the scars throughout the remainder of their lives.

A UNICEF study into the impact on children of 19 years of civil war in Afghanistan *(see also page 46)* found that trauma experienced by children in Kabul was chronic, influencing their emotional development, causing them to mistrust adults and feel deeply negative

---

[12] Minority Rights Group, War: *The Impact on Minority and Indigenous Children*, International Report, 1997/2.

[13] Coalition to Stop the use of Child Soldiers *Stop using Child Soldiers!* 1998.

[14] Daloni Carlisle, 'Child soldiers: Pulling back from the abyss'. Article in *Health Visitor*, UK, January 1998.

about their future. A disturbing 90 per cent believed they would die in the conflict. Many suffered from nightmares, anxiety, loss of appetite and concentration, and thought life not worth living.[15]

A similar study undertaken in Rwanda in 1996 (*see page* 36) found that more than two-thirds of children had actually witnessed someone being injured or killed.[16] Over 79 per cent had experienced a death in their immediate family – to which one- third were witness. Over 80 per cent had been forced to hide to protect themselves, of whom more than half hid for four to eight weeks or longer. No less than 16 per cent had hidden under dead bodies to survive. The magnitude of this trauma, and its impact on the children over their lifetimes, was inestimable, according to the psychologist who conducted the survey. Half the children still trembled or showed a strong physical reaction when reminded of these events more than a year later. Child victims of such horror and despair may carry forward an implacable spirit of hatred into the next generation unless they receive careful counselling and rehabilitation.

Even where its effects are less acute, day-to-day experience of pervasive conflict is quite different from that of an inter-state war. All community members, including children, are drawn into the effort as fighters or in other supporting roles. Violence imbues daily life. What the conflict is about, or where it is leading, typically becomes confused. Fact is indistinguishable from rumour and relations within communities – even families – are coloured by suspicion and mistrust. Fear of attack, and of localised acts of murder, arson, massacre, forced incarceration and forced displacement – acts sometimes covered by the phrase 'ethnic cleansing' – incites panic and flight.

Accumulative attacks and terrorisation of populations has caused flight on an unprecedented scale. Amnesty International estimates that there are 15 million refugees and 25-30 million internally displaced people. As a proportion of those fleeing their homes, the internally displaced have consistently increased.[17] Within both groups, around 50 per cent are children. Lacking the structure and nurture of their home communities, displaced children are more vulnerable to arbitrary

[15] Amnesty International, 'Afghanistan: Children traumatised by civil war'. South Asia Action for Children campaign, April 1998; from UNICEF's Psychosocial Assessment of Children Exposed to War-related Violence in Kabul, by Leila Gupta, Kabul, August 1997.
[16] UNICEF, Exposure to war-related violence among Rwandan children and adolescents, Leila Gupta, Kigali, February 1996.

action by those claiming authority over them, are more liable to suffer forced conscription or sexual abuse, and more regularly deprived of food, and such basic services as health care and education.[18]

Having been denied basic rights in their own communities, young people in flight are frequently also denied their rights by those whose protection is sought. In camps for the displaced, they may be targeted for recruitment as combatants or become prey to sexual assault. The state of insecurity in the surrounding countryside may mean freedom of movement is restricted, seriously reducing families' ability to cultivate land or find any means of survival. Such people may have no access to any judicial system – which may itself be seriously disrupted and fail to enforce laws which would normally be expected to protect children, their rights to life, property, and equal treatment.[19]

Child refugees accompanying their parents are often considered merely as dependants, and in camps for the displaced their special needs are overlooked. In other cases, parents flee without their children because of visa restrictions in countries where they are seeking asylum; it may subsequently prove impossible to reunite the family because the country of asylum refuses to admit them.[20] In the Russian Federation, families with children are being obstructed from gaining exit visas in order to seek asylum. In Pakistan, Afghan refugee children have been subject to arbitrary detention.[21]

In many countries, including Australia, Hong Kong, Japan, UK, and USA, children arriving with or without their families and seeking asylum have been arbitrarily detained in contravention of international human rights instruments. It is not unusual in some countries to find refugee children detained in prison-like conditions alongside convicted criminals. In some cases, detention can last many years. Some children of Vietnamese asylum-seekers were born and have grown up in detention centres in Hong Kong and Australia.[22]

The nature of today's conflicts thus generates an extremely high level of human and childhood rights abuse. And it exposes affected

---

[17] James Kunder, 'Internally displaced children: just scratching the surface', in *Internally Displaced People*, A global survey, Earthscan/Norwegian Refugee Council, 1998.
[18] Ibid.
[19] UNICEF Burundi, *Addressing the issue of child protection in Burundi*, Occasional Paper 02/97, August 1997
[20] Amnesty International, *A stolen future: Protecting the rights of refugee children*, July 1997.
[21] Amnesty International, *'Don't Play with my future!'* Appeal cases for International Children's Day, September 1997.

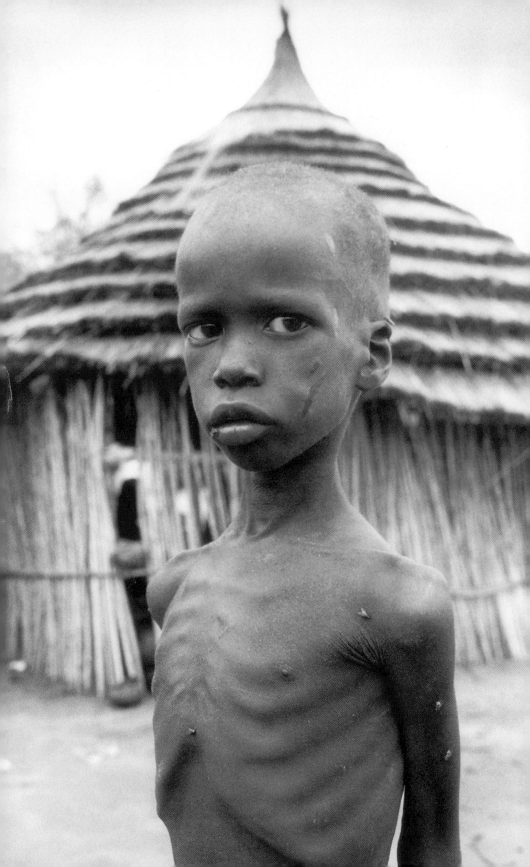

populations – adult and child – to threat of further rights violation stemming from the collapse of the social, governmental and administrative mechanisms on which their day-to-day lives and security depend.

Defending childhood rights

'Mankind owes the child the best it has to give.' From the 1959 Declaration on the Rights of the Child.

Since the proclamation of the Universal Declaration of Human Rights 50 years ago, a number of international instruments have further codified and defined these rights as they apply to all members of society, both in peacetime and in war. These include the 1951 UN Refugee Convention; the 1966 International Covenant on Civil and Political Rights; the 1987 Convention against Torture and Other Cruel, Inhuman or Degrading Treatment or Punishment; and the 1992 Declaration on the Rights of Persons belonging to National or Ethnic, Religious and Linguistic Minorities.

Awareness of the special forms of abuse and exploitation of children was heightened during the 1979 International Year of the Child. This led to a movement to codify and define the rights children should enjoy in addition to their rights as human beings. The notion of special childhood rights derives from their immaturity, and from their total dependency on adult structures of political and economic power to safeguard their well-being. Children do not only need protection against the potential failure of the adult world to meet their special needs. They also have the right to a say in adult decisions made on their behalf. Their youth may make them dependent on adults; but they are not merely adult chattels to be ordered at adult whim.

This concept of childhood has evolved and gained ground over the past 50 years, but it is still at odds with traditional norms in societies where the difference between adult *protection* and adult *property* is hazily, if at all, perceived. At its most extreme, the idea of children as the property of adults to use at will underlies the trafficking of Nepali children into brothels in India and elsewhere; the abductions of girls and boys by the LRA in northern Uganda; involuntary female genital mutilation in many parts of Africa and some countries of the Middle East; and forced marriages of young girls in parts of Asia and Latin

Famine, a product of war. Southern Sudan. August 1998.
© Jenny Matthews

'Anti-personnel' = 'anti-children'

The growth of anti-personnel weapon technology has made both war and peace more dangerous for children. Millions of the 'anti-personnel' landmines lying unexploded in Cambodia, Afghanistan, Angola, Bosnia, Vietnam, Somalia, Iraq and elsewhere, were spread on or near roads, tracks and footpaths – usually in the countryside. Millions of others were dropped from the air as 'cluster bombs', covering huge areas of land with tiny explosives waiting to be detonated by anyone passing by – soldier or civilian, adult or child.

Long after the end of a conflict, these weapons kill. The UN estimates there are over 100 million unexploded mines in the world. In Angola, 9 million mines amount to one for every person in the country. In 30 countries, mines constitute a

America. There is a deep contradiction in the dependency of children: how can a child be simultaneously old enough to kill or be sexually used at adult behest, and too young to have a say in matters governing his or her life?

Although the rights perspective on childhood is still not universally understood or accepted, it has been expressed and codified in a set of standards which now enjoy an unprecedented standing among human rights instruments. The Convention on the Rights of the Child was passed by the UN General Assembly in 1989, and so swiftly ratified by the requisite number of countries as to pass into international law within a year. The Convention has since become the most fully ratified human rights instrument in history: only the USA and the collapsed state of Somalia are lagging. Some *de facto* authorities which remain legally unrecognised also acknowledge it.[23]

During the 1990s, organisations such as UNICEF, Save the Children, Radda Barnen, and Amnesty International, and a host of other NGOs, have popularised the idea of child rights and the Convention within countries all over the world. Some developing

humanitarian crisis as they kill or injure around 24,000 men, women and children every year. Children are especially susceptible, and the tasks given to children – gathering firewood, tending animal herds or collecting water – make it more likely they will disturb unexploded mines.

These weapons were laid or dropped in full knowledge that their likely 'target' will be civilians, often children, that they will make areas extremely dangerous for years to come – areas which poor people will have to farm after the war. The deliberate cruelty of anti-personnel mines prompted an unprecedented campaign to ban them, leading to the 1997 Mine Ban Treaty[24] prohibiting their use, export and manufacture, now signed by 130 countries including the UK.

Determined to put an end to the suffering and casualties by anti-personnel mines, that kill or maim hundreds of people every week, mostly innocent and defenceless civilians and especially children...

Opening Paragraph of the Preamble to the Mine Ban Treaty[25]

The legacy of landmines will take years to overcome, but the campaign's success stemmed from its ambitious demand for a total ban on anti-personnel mines. The campaign sought to stigmatise any use of anti-personnel mines as they are an undeniably cruel weapon. Stigmatisation among the world community of an established military tactic has been a powerful catalyst for change.[26]

countries have set up Child Rights Forums to promote children's rights and tackle the obstructions – legal, institutional, economic, social and attitudinal – which inhibit their fulfilment. The involvement of children's own organisations, which have been encouraged to develop and use their own voices in defence of their rights, is an important characteristic of many campaigns for child rights promotion.

The Convention provides a framework of international law within which to analyse the fulfilment of childhood rights, and a means of holding States Parties responsible for violations of those rights. It has also become a vehicle for changing attitudes – state, community, and

[23] ODI, Iain Levine, *Promoting humanitarian principles: the southern Sudan experience*, Relief and Rehabilitation Network paper No. 21, May 1997.
[24] The Mine Ban Treaty is formally called 'The Convention on the Prohibition of the Use, Stockpiling, Production and Transfer of Anti-Personnel Mines and On Their Destruction'.
[25] The full text of the Mine Ban Treaty is on the website of the International Campaign to Ban Landmines: http://www.icbl.org/
[26] Eric Prokosch, *The Technology of Killing – a military and political history of antipersonnel weapons*, Zed Books, 1995.

parental – towards children and childhood, including the attitude that children 'should be seen, but not be heard'.

In situations of conflict, especially those characterised by random violence and lawlessness, the upholding of children's rights is at its most problematic. A retreat into armed confrontation means the collapse of the rule of law and of the use of dialogue and negotiation for human defence. Even where conflict has ended, or at least temporarily receded from the national stage, it can be extremely difficult to re-establish systems of childhood protection. The authorities may feel insecure and inclined to arbitrary action, as in Turkey, Sri Lanka, or Colombia. Or they may fail to dismantle the state machinery of violent oppression used during an overt conflict and let it continue to wreak its extra-judicial, destructive force.[27]

Conflict swells the numbers of children in special need – the orphaned, children on the streets, children sold or trafficked, juveniles perceived as threatening to authority. And society's battered institutions may have fewer resources to help rebuild their lives. Like many human rights instruments, the Convention provides an 'armour of right' that is not impregnable. It can be held up as a benchmark of behaviour towards children and a framework within which to establish policy and change national law, but it cannot ultimately force national governments to change.

However, the Convention derives huge moral strength from its near-universal ratification and the widespread popularisation of its standards. Where state authorities, including armies and security forces, are responsible for child rights violations, the governments of the countries concerned can be internationally admonished through the Convention monitoring process. The Committee on the Rights of the Child, the expert body responsible for the Convention's implementation, encourages States Parties via a process of dialogue to take steps to reduce such violations. In the wake of strife, incoming authorities or *de facto* powers can sometimes be persuaded to make a public commitment to fulfilment of child rights as a demonstration of their desire to build a better society.

Even in the case of internal conflicts, it has proved possible in some instances – in 1994 in southern Sudan for example – to persuade warlords to adhere to principles of childhood protection set out in the Convention.[28] In other simmering or stop-go conflict settings, such as

---

[27] AI, *Guatemala: State of impunity*, op cit.

Sri Lanka, Lebanon, Palestine and Burundi, the Convention has been used as a basis for public education activities to promulgate values of childhood protection, mutual understanding, and peace. It is also a useful instrument for the establishment of standards and programmes in camps for the displaced; and for the protection of children affected by conflict who have become vulnerable to further rights violations – through being orphaned, for example.

The application of the Convention can take many forms. Certain articles deal specifically with the situation of children affected by armed conflict; these are the articles mainly cited in negotiations between humanitarian organisations and the warring parties. Article 38 asserts children's right to protection in time of war, including their right not to be recruited into the armed forces, or take part in hostilities. The minimum age of recruitment is set at 15, but there is growing support for an optional protocol to the Convention to raise it to 18, Article 22 establishes special rights for child refugees.[29] There are also provisions for the aftermath of conflict. Article 22 asserts, for those separated from their parents, the right to efforts on their behalf to locate relatives and bring about family reunification. Article 39 asserts the right of children injured, abused, exploited, traumatised or disabled during war to special care and treatment to aid their recovery and rehabilitation into society.

However, there are many applications of the Convention far more extensive than these specific protections for children in war. Many of the general situations of child need and loss of protection envisaged by the Convention are especially likely to arise where people are terrorised, uprooted, and physically attacked. Relevant articles include Article 9, covering the forcible separation of children from their parents; Article 10, covering the right of a child to leave, or enter, a country; and Article 20, concerning children without families.

Protection from gross abuse and exploitation is also addressed in several Articles. Article 19 asserts the child's right to protection from violence, injury or abuse; Article 34 covers protection against sexual exploitation; Article 35 covers abduction, sale or trafficking; and Article 37 covers torture or cruel and degrading treatment.

Another important set of rights covered by the Convention may be indirectly violated in a state of conflict or political insecurity. These are

---

[28] *Promoting humanitarian principles: the southern Sudan experience*, op cit.
[29] UNICEF, *First Call for Children: The Convention on the Rights of the Child*, New York, 1990.

the child's right to non-discrimination on grounds of race, sex, language, political or religious belief (Article 2), to survival and development (Article 6), to food, water, and health care (Article 24), to education (Article 28), to recreation (Article 31); and to the means of cultural and spiritual development including the right to practise his or her religion (Article 30). These rights cannot be met by standard fire brigade relief aid, and they include services essential to foster children's physical, intellectual and psycho-social development.

For all three groups of rights, violations are much more likely to occur when a child has become separated from his or her family, in the thick of fighting, by orphanhood, or during flight. The absence of adult protectors whose primary concern towards the child is his or her well-being deprives the child of a protective shield against further violations. Given the strong ethnic component of many conflicts and insurrections, if a child belongs to an ethnic or religious minority or an indigenous group, this will add to the risk factors.[30]

Where poverty rather than ethnicity is at the root of systems of social hierarchy, as in parts of Latin America and Asia, this is also a compounding factor. Arbitrary actions against children by state authorities in countries such as Brazil and Venezuela are almost invariably against children from the barrios or economically disadvantaged groups.[31] In parts of India and elsewhere in South Asia, it is common for police to pick up children for minor offences, such as begging and vagrancy, and ill-treat and even torture them before sending them on to observation homes.[32] Their presence on the street may identify them as coming from a socially inferior group, to be regarded as a public nuisance against whom punitive action is regarded as legitimate, instead of as children in need of special protection and care.

Peace and the child rights culture

An important reason for highlighting abuses of children's rights associated with conflict or violent acts of state repression is to instil in the public mind a sense of the damage being done to childhood. Too often, human rights offences come across as the isolated acts of psychopaths or evil individuals, which all 'normal' human beings and authorities naturally deplore. However, once documented, they may

---

[30] *War: The Impact on Minority and Indigenous Children*, op cit.
[31] *Venezuela, The silent cry*, op cit.

become exposed as a pattern supported by pseudo-cultural values and behavioural norms. These are the self-same values and norms which perpetuate conflict and unrest, creating a society in which mutual distrust and hatred between different groups become ever more entrenched.

Promoting a culture of human rights is a means of holding up a mirror for society to judge its attitudes and behaviour. Children's

'What happened to my son today – will it not happen to others tomorrow?'

This is a question asked by the mother of a 13-year-old boy tortured at a police station in Istanbul[33]. Protections for children in police custody exist in Turkish law but are frequently ignored. Given police threats and financial inducement against parents who lodge complaints, any mother – especially from an ethnic minority background – who carries forward an official protest on her child's behalf will require exceptional courage. But the process of revelation and calling violators to public account is essential to the promotion of a child rights culture, as this testimony underlines.

vulnerability and defencelessness make this self-judgment easier – and should bring compensatory action in the form of new policies and better implementation. Promoting the well-being of children has always been a cause around which disparate groups can coalesce: few voices will ever be raised against it. Growing recognition of the need to protect child rights can jump-start a process of attitudinal change and institutional and legal reform. This has been the logic behind calls by leading advocates on behalf of children for child rights to be made the cutting-edge of human rights.[34]

There are different ways in which promoting the culture of rights could reduce damage to childhood caused directly or indirectly by conflict. The typical response of humanitarian organisations is to move beyond instant relief, and institute programmes to restore the full range of basic services, including psychosocial counselling and trauma recovery. Some organisations, notably the Red Cross, have

---

[32] *South Asia: Action for Children*, op cit.
[33] Amnesty International, *Turkey: Children at risk of torture, death in custody and 'disappearance'*, November 1996.
[34] James P. Grant, UNICEF Executive Director, *Children's rights: the Cutting Edge of Human Rights*. Speech at the World Conference on Human Rights, June 1993.

Unaccompanied Rwandan Hutu children on board a cargo plane home to Kigali, Rwanda, after their refugee camp was attacked 1997.

© Howard Davies

specialised in tracing the relatives of unaccompanied children and reuniting families. Removing landmines and mine awareness programmes have also become a vital component of humanitarian work in present and former conflict zones.

As well as programmatic responses, many NGOs and some international organisations also undertake advocacy of child rights. This is frequently on an issue-by-issue basis. The campaign against landmines which led to the 1997 Ottawa Treaty banning their manufacture and use is the best-known example of the impact of advocacy on a specific children-and-war-related issue. Currently, a coalition of organisations including Amnesty International is trying to end the use of children as soldiers.[35]

Exposing more localised abuses is also vital. This is where the work of Amnesty International comes into its own. By advancing the cause of specific groups of children affected by conflict – refugee groups, those seeking asylum, child victims of arbitrary arrest and extra-judicial action – Amnesty International exposes the way in which States Parties to the Convention and other relevant conventions are failing to live up to the obligations towards children they have committed themselves to uphold.

By amassing witness reports to individual cases of gross child rights violation, Amnesty International may help bring the violators to book, as a group or as individuals. Over time, this may bring combatants and security forces to understand the consequences of their actions not only for 'enemy' children but for their own, and help create an environment in which those who have been brutalised or socialised to violence can be rehabilitated and their childhoods repaired.

Promoting the culture of rights has been an important outcome of the passage into international law of the Convention. With the 50th anniversary of the Universal Declaration of Human Rights, advancing the cause of human rights by awareness-raising, calling violators to account, and lobbying for legislative reform are in themselves means to build peace throughout the family of humankind. Within that overall purpose, advancing the rights of children demands a special place.

---

[35] *Stop using Child Soldiers!* op cit.

2

Hidden casualties of conflict

Robert Beasley

'To destroy the big rats, you must kill the little rats'

Radio Libre Mille Collines broadcast, April 1994, encouraging Hutu militia to target Tutsi children.

In 'modern' wars of attrition, millions of civilians, mainly women and children, have been shot, shelled, bombed, blasted and bullied from their homes. Civilian war casualties have increased from five per cent in the First World War, to over 90 per cent in the 1990s: the overwhelming majority are women and children.

Buried in the seven-digit statistics are individual stories. On average, more than 2,000 children have been killed, maimed or disabled by war *every day* over the past decade. Landmines kill and maim 800 children every month – often exploding years after the 'end' of a conflict (*see page 22*). Technological advances in weaponry, such as cluster bombs and fuel-air weapons, make indiscriminate killing of civilians easier. Terror tactics have caused massive movements of refugees in Europe, Africa, Latin America, the Middle East and Asia. Up to 14 million children have lost their homes and sought refuge in camps or cities or – for the few – another country.

Government forces frequently treat entire populations as suspect – often the very populations they claim to represent, and especially teenagers and young adults. Sexual exploitation and rape is a continual threat to women and particularly adolescent girls during armed conflict. Murder and torture have been long denounced as war crimes. Rape, usually downplayed as an inevitable side effect of war, is used as a tactical weapon to terrorise populations and put them to flight.[36]

---

[36] UN, *The Impact of Armed Conflict on Children*, Graça Machel Report to UN General Assembly, 26 August 1996.

Coffin of a street child killed by death squads. Recife, Brazil

© Carlos Reyes-Manzo

How war hurts children

Even when children are not directly injured during armed conflicts, the fallout affects them in many different ways.

- *Nutritional deprivation*: conflicts often cause famines, with food production and distribution systems destroyed or disrupted.
- *Spread of disease*: communicable diseases are the major cause of death among children in peacetime. In wars, the risks multiply as water and food supplies are damaged and health services disrupted.
- *Psychological damage*: especially if children have directly witnessed or been involved in acts of violence.
- *Disability*: Around 4 million child survivors of conflicts in the past decade have been permanently disabled and landmines continue to kill and maim.
- *Loss of education*: Schools are frequently closed in wars, and are even destroyed as a key part of the social fabric. Displacement adds to further disruption.
- *Child combatants*: Children who have lost their parents or who come from disrupted families are more likely to become soldiers.
- *Violence against girls*: Rape is featured in almost every armed conflict and is common in camps of the displaced. In some conflicts, rape is used as a systematic weapon of terror.
- *Child abduction, torture and slavery*: Children kidnapped by armies are frequently beaten and either forcibly enlisted as combatants or enslaved.
- *Child war criminals*: Children are often involved in acts of violence. Sometimes this may be a deliberate tactic to ensure communal complicity in atrocities. Psychological damage through involvement in such acts may be acute.[37]

Genocide and after

When the killing of Rwandan Tutsis began in April 1994, few observers expected it to reach its genocidal conclusion. In 100 days, up to one million men, women and children were dead, most killed by Hutu militia mobs aligned to the Rwandan government. They shot, and hacked people to death with machetes at the rate of around 10,000 human beings a day.

Throughout the slaughter, Hutus were urged to kill anyone who was Tutsi, or anyone opposing the slaughter. The extremist radio station Radio Mille Collines broadcast genocidal messages throughout the

---

[37] UNICEF UK, *Children in Conflict – a child rights emergency*, Maggie Black, 1998.

killing. No-one was spared, least of all Tutsi children. The militia deliberately involved entire communities in the slaughter. Children were used to pick out Tutsis and were expected to join in the killings. By 1997, 2,000 children were detained on suspicion of acts of genocide.

And when the mainly-Tutsi Rwandan Patriotic Front gradually gained the upper hand and pushed out the Hutu government forces, Hutu children joined the exodus. Hundreds of thousands of Hutus ended up finding 'sanctuary' in makeshift refugee camps in Zaire (now the Democratic Republic of Congo) and Tanzania – where the *Interahamwe* Hutu militia remained active.

The camps in Zaire became the scene of terrible battles two years later in 1996, when rebel forces attacked with shells and mortars. Rebel troops of the *Alliance des forces démocratiques pour la libération du Congo-Zaïre* (AFDL) killed unarmed refugees, including the very young and very old. Indiscriminate bombardments forced over half a million people to move. Most returned to Rwanda, despite their fears of the RPF government. At least 40,000 fled into Tanzania. Unknown numbers simply fled into the forests to fend for themselves.

Attacks by the AFDL continued. Cases of 'disappearance', torture, rape, arbitrary arrest and unlawful detention were reported. The main targets were members of the Hutu ethnic group – mainly refugees from Rwanda, but also those from neighbouring Burundi and Congolese nationals.

Then in April 1997, the AFDL blocked access to large refugee camps south of Kisingani. Aid workers were allowed in for just two hours a day, supposedly for their own protection, while up to 70 people a day died from malnutrition and disease – especially the more vulnerable like children and the elderly. The reasons for the obstruction became clear in late April 1997, when as many as 40,000 Rwandan refugees 'disappeared' from the camps. Attacks on Biaro camp began on 22 April. By 23 April it was deserted. Women survivors who found shelter in nearby forests said that boys and men had been separated from them by AFDL soldiers; moments later, they heard gunshots.

On 26 April 1997, AFDL forces abducted 52 Hutu refugee children who were in the Lwiro hospital receiving treatment for illness and malnutrition. The children were kept in a closed container, beaten and denied food and drink for three days. An international outcry led to their return to the hospital in a 'pretty bad condition', according to

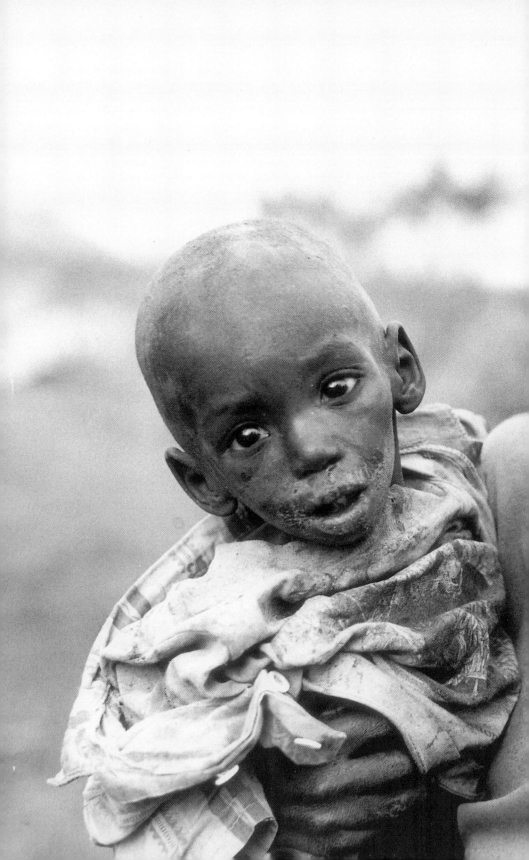

UNICEF. As many as 200 Rwandan refugees were reportedly killed on 13 May 1997 by members of the AFDL in and around Mbandaka, in the Equateur region. Witnesses said a further 140 refugees were killed by the AFDL at nearby Wenji. AFDL soldiers reportedly held children by the legs and smashed their heads against the ground or trees. On 29 May 1997, four Rwandan refugees, including a child, and a Congolese Save the Children Fund worker were shot dead by AFDL troops at Karuba. The Save the Children Fund worker, Katumbo Mburanumwe, was carrying the child on his back when they were both shot.[38]

Exposure to war-related violence among Rwandan children and adolescents

Traumatic event	% of children*
Witnessed violence	95.5
Experienced death in the family	79.6
Witnessed someone being killed or injured	69.5
Were threatened with death	61.5
Believed they would die	90.6
Witnessed killings or injuries with 'pangas' (machetes)	57.7
Witnessed rape or sexual assault	31.4
Saw dead bodies or parts of bodies	87.5
Witnessed massacre	51.9
Hid for protection	80.2

* (n = 3,030) aged 8-19, half in centres, half in the community
Source: UNICEF, *Exposure to War Related Violence among Rwandan Children and Adolescents: A Brief Report on the National Baseline Trauma Survey*, Leila Gupta, Rwanda, February 1996.

The lasting impact on the children of Rwanda is hard to imagine. A UNICEF survey of children in Kigali in 1996 found they had been exposed to extraordinary horror during the conflict. Over half had witnessed massacres. Ninety per cent had believed they would be killed. Eight out of ten had lost family members in the violence. More

---

[38] Amnesty International, *Democratic Republic of Congo: Deadly Alliances in Congolese forests*, 3 December 1997.

than one in six had only survived by hiding underneath corpses, often the corpses of their own family and friends.[39]

Those Hutu children involved in the genocide will have their own traumas, which for many will be compounded by repeated flight as refugees.

'We are trying to teach them to trust the world again, but it is very, very difficult.'

Rose Kayitesi, running an orphanage in Byumba, Rwanda, 1994.[40]

'The Interahamwe (Hutu militia) came to our house and they asked all who are inyenzi (cockroaches) to step outside...I followed my parents and brothers and sisters out into the fields at the back and we ran. But they ran fast and caught us and they killed my family members and they thought they had killed me too. They hit me with the machetes and clubs and then threw all the bodies together so that I was lying under my mother who was dead. But I was not dead...'

Orphaned survivor, Byumba, Rwanda, 1994.[41]

Caught in the conflict

In Algeria, thousands of children have been killed, injured and traumatised by the conflict between government security forces and armed groups calling themselves 'Islamic groups'.

On the night of 22-23 September 1997, more than 200 people, including many children, were massacred in the village Bentalha, a few kilometres south of Algiers. Bentalha is near five different army and security forces outposts. Two main army barracks are just a few kilometres away and several security forces posts are only a few hundreds metres away. Survivors said that at the time of the massacre armed forces units with armoured vehicles were stationed outside the village – just a few hundreds metres from the place where the massacre was taking place. They did not intervene to stop the killings or arrest

---

[39] UNICEF, *Exposure to war-related violence among Rwandan children and adolescents*, Leila Gupta, Kigali, February 1996. *(See page 115:* AI reports on Rwanda 1990-96).
[40] Feargal Keane: *Season of Blood, a Rwandan journey*, Viking 1995.
[41] Feargal Keane: *Season of Blood, a Rwandan journey*, Viking 1995.

the perpetrators, who were able to leave undisturbed. The killers spent several hours in Bentalha; they slaughtered, decapitated and mutilated men, women and children. Some of the children were snatched from their parents' arms and killed in front of them; others were murdered and thrown off balconies. Those who survived saw their parents, relatives and neighbours die.

Children have witnessed the killing of parents or neighbours. Children have had parents killed or abducted either by security forces or by armed groups. Children have witnessed bomb explosions, military operations by the army and security forces, and attacks by armed groups.

One night at the end of February 1995 Malika, Rachid and Omar (not their real names), aged between six and 12, woke up when a group of men came to kill their father. Then, the men tied their mother's hands, and killed her. Then they killed a female neighbour who had helped their mother during a previous attack. The children's father was a policeman, their mother a housewife. Their father had received death threats against him and his family, and there had been previous attempts to kill him. Armed opposition 'Islamic groups' often kill civilian relatives of members of the security forces.

Samira (not her real name), aged six, was asleep when security forces came to the family home in May 1996 and killed four of her uncles, and her grandfather, aged 84. They made her uncles lie on the floor and shot them in the back of the head. Her grandfather screamed and they shot him in the face, in front of Samira. Before leaving they also shot the dog, which survived. Samira's uncles and grandfather were ordinary people, but another uncle was a member of an armed Islamist group, and was on the run. The Algerian security forces often kill civilian relatives of members of armed opposition groups.[42]

In the name of the Lord

Children living in the Gulu and Kitgum districts of northern Uganda have been targeted since 1994 by soldiers belonging to the Lord's Resistance Army (LRA), a self-styled rebel group fighting the Ugandan government.

Up to 8,000 children have been systematically abducted and forced to join the LRA. Most of them have been between 13 and 16 years old. Younger children are not usually strong enough to carry weapons or

---

[42] Amnesty International, *Algeria: Children Caught in the Conflict*, 27 October 1997.

loads, while older children are less malleable to the will of their abductors. Children are beaten, murdered and forced to fight well-armed government troops. They are chattels 'owned' by the LRA leadership. Girls are raped and used as sexual slaves. The forced marriage of girls is the cornerstone of the LRA's incentive structure.

Those abducted are forced to abuse others, both inside and outside the LRA. The LRA terrorises villagers: thousands of civilians in northern Uganda have been killed; thousands of women have been raped. The killers and rapists themselves are often abused children. This is deliberate. The children are often traumatised by what they have done and feel they are outcasts. They become more closely bound to the LRA.[43]

Children's welfare is also destroyed in other ways. The LRA has targeted schools, killing at least 70 teachers in Kitgum district between 1993 and July 1996. In July and August 1996, 11 teachers and over 100 children were killed by the LRA in Gulu district. LRA raiders included boys from the school under attack. The LRA feeds itself by looting or by forcing villagers to hand over food. Communities which resist the LRA or who are suspected of working with the Ugandan government are punished.

On 20 April 1995, the LRA attacked Atiak, a trading centre north of Gulu. Several hundred people were rounded up and marched about six miles south west to the banks of a river. The captives were divided into categories: children under 11, the elderly, pregnant and breastfeeding mothers, and young men and women, including children over the age of 11. The LRA commander is reported to have accused the civilians of not proving support to the movement. At midday, the adolescents and young adults were shot dead. Over 130 were killed by the river bank, including over 40 students from Atiak Technical College.[44]

The Lord's Resistance Army has not published an understandable political program, beyond calling for Uganda to be ruled according to the biblical Ten Commandments. But its edicts paint a picture of medieval ferocity, where riding a bicycle is punished by amputation and habitation near roads is prohibited, as is keeping pigs. The latter appears to be a sop to the LRA's backers, the current Islamist government in Sudan.

---

[43] Amnesty International, *Uganda: Breaking God's Commands – the destruction of childhood by the Lord's Resistance Army*, 18 September 1997.
[44] AI, *Uganda: Breaking God's Commands....*, 18 September 1997.

Faced with the LRA's attacks, much of the population has fled. By mid-1997, about 50 per cent of the population of Gulu district had fled their homes – about 200,000 people – and sought sanctuary in towns, outlying trading centres or small army posts in so-called protected villages. Around 60,000 have been displaced in Kitgum district.

Abducted for slavery

With a landmass the size of Western Europe, Sudan is geographically awesome. Over the past decade, its record for human rights violations has been on a shocking scale.

A bitter civil war between the Islamist government and factions of the Sudan People's Liberation Army (which also fight each other) has left thousands dead with civilians as the main victims.

In government operations in a largely hidden war in Bahr al-Ghazal in southern Sudan, attacks on civilians have included their apparent abduction to be sold into slavery. In an area racked by famine, desperate civilians have moved near the strategically important railway line to Wau, as some trains carry vital food supplies.

But other trains reap a different harvest. As government trains make their way along the line, outriders on horseback from the Popular Defence Force (PDF) have fanned out and attacked villages and settlements in the neighbouring countryside. On their way they have killed adults, abducted children, destroyed standing crops and stolen cattle.

In April 1993, Apiu Majok, 12, and her sister, Acuir, nine, were among a number of girls abducted by PDF troops from the Luo village of Pankuel, in northern Bahr-al-Ghazal. Terrified, they were put on a northbound government train which was carrying a number of other children. Acuir Majok was released when regular police intervened at Aweil, the main garrison town in northern Bahr al-Ghazal. Although far from her home, Acuir was more fortunate than her sister, who was never seen again.

Apiu is one of 300 women and children abducted as this train passed down and up the line. Many were freed when the train reached Aweil. But many others were not. No action appears to have been taken against the PDF troops responsible for the abductions. When another government train travelled along the same line in June and July 1993, murders, rapes and abductions by PDF horsemen were again widespread. In February 1994, the UN Special Rapporteur on Sudan reported that this train was carrying 217 abducted children by the time it arrived in Wau. Local authorities there did nothing to intervene. When the train travelled north, authorities in Aweil and Korrok freed 169 children. Eighty children kidnapped onto this train were not seen again. It is widely assumed they were sold into domestic slavery.[45] The Sudanese authorities took no action against those responsible for their 'disappearance'.

> *'The train was going north. The PDF caught me in the forest with cows and goats. They beat me a bit and then they dragged me towards Aweil. Then they reached Kuom they started putting little children in sacks. I was locked in a lavatory with five boys. I knew three... In Aweil there was a search by police. They found us and we were freed.'*

Sudanese youth, abducted by the PDF in July 1993.[46]

Destruction of Yugoslavia

In the wars that sprung up during the disintegration of Yugoslavia, entire population groups were targeted by one or other side. Between 1991 and 1995, around 2.5 million people were displaced from or within Bosnia-Herzegovina and Croatia. Armed forces from all sides made little or no attempt to distinguish between soldiers and civilians. 'Ethnic cleansing' entered the lexicon of modern warfare. Thousands were 'disappeared' and the discovery of secret mass graves after the fighting have slowly revealed their fate. Women and adolescent girls were subjected to rape as a deliberate tactic – to terrorise civilian populations into flight.

Throughout 1998, ethnic Albanians in Kosovo fled Serbian police, army and paramilitary forces who swept through on the offensive against the Kosovo Liberation Army (KLA), an armed group fighting for Kosovan independence from Yugoslavia. Police targeted houses, regardless of the fact that often women, children and unarmed men were sheltering in them.[47]

Such indiscriminate attacks are typical of strategies to terrorise civilian populations into flight. In a Serbian forces operation on 5 and

---

[45] Amnesty International, *Sudan: 'The Tears of Orphans'– No future without human rights*, January 1995.

[46] Amnesty International, *Sudan Campaign – Appeal Cases*,1995, p29-30.

[47] Amnesty International, See *Human Rights Crisis in Kosovo* series 1-4,1998.

6 March 1998 at the village of Donji Prekaz, in the Drenica region of Kosovo, at least 54 people were killed, including nine children aged between 8 and 16 from one extended family. The 'target' of the raid was a member of this family who had been convicted *in absentia* of 'terrorism' in July 1997.

The KLA has also engaged in tactics designed to force out Serbs who live in Kosovo, such as hostage taking and the arbitrary killing of civilians.

Tens of thousands of Kosovans have fled the fighting. A few have reached the safety of countries like Britain. Several thousand have sought refuge in Bosnia-Herzegovina. But up to 200,000 refugees – mostly women and children – have sought sanctuary inside the borders of the Federal Republic of Yugoslavia, where their protection and welfare is precarious.

An uncivil war

Children have been particular victims of violence in Sierra Leone, where internal armed conflict continued after a military coup on 25 May 1997. But the restoration of the overthrown government of President Kabbah in March 1998 did not bring peace. Thousands of children have been arbitrarily killed, mutilated, maimed, abducted and forced to fight by the rebel forces of the ousted Armed Forces Revolutionary Council (AFRC) and Revolutionary United Front (RUF). Girls and women have been systematically raped and forced into sexual slavery.

After April 1998, the AFRC and RUF began *Operation no living thing*, a systematic campaign of killing, rape and mutilation. Many hundreds of men, women and children of all ages have suffered mutilation and crude amputations of their arms, legs, lips or ears, lacerations and gunshot wounds. Women and girls have been raped or suffered other forms of sexual assault. Survivors of attacks who manage to reach safety and medical assistance recount that many others from their villages were killed or fled into the bush, their fate unknown.

A 15-year-old schoolboy from Koidu, in Kono District, Eastern Province, who reached the Connaught Hospital in Freetown on 10 May 1998, had suffered severe lacerations to his right ankle from an attempted amputation. Almost 50 people with him had been killed when they were attacked on 1 May 1998.

Three young women survived an attack on the village of Boima in

Bombali District, Northern Province, on 7 May 1998; one had a deep cut to her arm, the other two had been beaten all over their bodies. One of the women had witnessed the killing of several members of her family, including her children. Twelve people, including three of her children, died when their house was set alight. Another child, a girl aged three, was pulled from her back and cut with machetes.

Among more than 350,000 Sierra Leoneans who have either become refugees in neighbouring countries or internally displaced since February 1998 are hundreds of unaccompanied children separated from their families as a result of the violence. Children are the most vulnerable to the acute hardship, disease and malnutrition faced by Sierra Leonean refugees and displaced people. During May and June 1998, 750 people, including children, were reported to have died of disease and malnutrition at Masingbi, in Tonkolili District, Northern Province, where some 15,000 displaced people sought safety.[48]

Killing in Colombia

Around one tenth of the world's murders take place in Colombia, where a long-running guerrilla war, drug smuggling and counter-insurgency operations have produced a wave of violence.

Up to 1,000,000 people – mainly women and children – live as 'internally-displaced people' in Colombia. They have fled violence in their home areas – typically fleeing from the Colombian army and right-wing paramilitary groups who treat civilians in 'guerrilla areas' as suspects and thus targets. Massacres are common. When a military operation descended on the El Bosque community in Riofrío, Valle de Cauca department, in October 1993, 13 people were dragged from their homes, tortured and killed: 12 of the victims were from the Ladino and Molina families, four of them children aged 15 or 16.[49] Colombian military commanders claimed the 13 were 'guerrillas killed in combat'. Among those similarly targeted as 'guerrillas' are trade unionists, lawyers and human rights activists.

'They grabbed me and threw me on the floor. Papi also. Then they made us stand up. I told them that this was my Papi and they

---

[48] Amnesty International, *Sierra Leone: The UN special conference on Sierra Leone...*, 24 July 1998. See also *Sierra Leone: 1998 – a year of atrocities against civilians.*
[49] Amnesty International, *Just what do we have to do to stay alive? – Colombia's internally displaced*, 1 October 1997; and *Colombia: Children and minors – victims of political violence*, June 1994.

shouldn't harm him or me because there were lots of young
children and if they killed my Papi, I would be left to care for them
alone. They told me I should go home and I started out for the
house immediately. They killed Papi soon after.'

A young boy describing an army raid on his home in Urabá in 1995, which left him orphaned
and homeless.[50]

Some 75 per cent of the displaced in Colombia are under 25 years
old; several thousands are heads of families because of the death of
one or both parents. Families in Colombia also flee from their homes
to avoid the forced conscription of their children, male and female,
sometimes as young as 13, by guerilla groups. A 'volunteer' is often
requested from every family with more than one child.

Torturing children

In Turkey, Amnesty International has recorded children as young as 12
being subjected to torture, including electric shocks, hosing with cold
water and beating. Children as young as 14 have reported being
sexually assaulted and threatened with rape.

Döne Talun, a 12-year-old girl, was tortured in Ankara Police
Headquarters for five days. She was said to have stolen some bread.
She was beaten and given electric shocks. Although her family filed a
complaint – and although the incommunicado detention and
interrogation of minors are illegal in Turkish law – prosecutors
decided not to prosecute her torturers.[51]

Torture is systematic in Turkey. The European Committee for the
Prevention of Torture reported in December 1992 that – when it
visited the Ankara Police HQ – they found 'a low stretcher-type bed
equipped with eight straps (four each side), fitting perfectly the
description of the item of furniture to which persons had said they
were secured when electric shocks were administered to them. No
credible explanation could be proffered for the presence of this bed in
what was indicated by a sign as being an *interrogation room*'.[52]

Children have also 'disappeared' after eyewitnesses last saw them

[50] Amnesty International, *Just what do we have to do to stay alive?* 1 October 1997.
[51] Amnesty International, *Turkey: Children at risk of torture, death in custody and
'disappearance'*, 20 November 1996, and *Turkey – No security without human rights*,
October 1996.
[52] Amnesty International, Report of European Committee for the Prevention of Torture,
quoted in *Turkey – No security without human rights*, October 1996.

A beating looms for a child as he searches for food. Bombay, 1994.

© Dario Mitidieri

being taken away by security forces. In the conflict between the Kurdish Workers' Party (PKK) and state forces in the southeast, children have been victims of abuses by both sides. Children have been killed in village massacres committed by the PKK, but also in operations by state security forces.

Poverty, hunger, persecution

South Asia's 539 million children (under 18) make up over 40 per cent of the population, and a quarter of the world's children. Over half of under-fives are 'moderately or seriously underweight' because of inadequate diet.[53] But malnutrition is only one of their hurdles: they face a catalogue of human rights violations at the hands of state agencies and armed opposition groups – from arbitrary detention, cruel punishments and torture to killings and 'disappearance' in armed conflict.[54]

In Sri Lanka, scores of children aged from a few months to 17 years are among thousands who have 'disappeared' after being detained by security forces or armed groups engaged over the past 15 years. Jeganathan Janagan, a 17-year-old student, 'disappeared' after being taken from his home at Nailur, Jaffna, at around 2am on 14 July 1996. Pranaban Kumaraswamy 'disappeared' in September 1996 after making inquiries about the 'disappearance of his sister. Pranaban's body was found a few weeks later in a shallow grave. On one day in September 1990, 68 Tamil children 'disappeared' after being detained in Batticaloa by Sri Lankan army soldiers. It is feared they were murdered. As of March 1998, no-one had been prosecuted for their 'disappearance'. 'Disappearances' in Sri Lanka continue to take place, especially in Jaffna where the army is fighting Tamil separatists.

During 19 years of bitter civil conflict in Afghanistan, thousands of children have been killed in deliberate or indiscriminate attacks on their homes, schools or playing fields. Hundreds of others have been subjected to torture, including rape, at the hand of the numerous armed political groups.

In September 1997, around 70 civilians including children were murdered by armed guards of one warring faction in Qezelabad village near Mazar-e Sharif. Survivors said the perpetrators were *Taleban* guards. *Taleban* officials deny this. All the victims belonged to the Hazara minority. Among them was a boy of about eight who was reportedly killed and decapitated. Other reports stated that victims had their eyes gouged out with bayonets. Two boys of about 12 were reportedly held by the guards and had their arms and hands broken with stones.[55] In August 1998, many children were among the thousands of ethnic Hazara civilians deliberately and systematically killed by Taleban guards in the days following their military take over of Mazare Sharif.

Almost every family in Afghanistan has been affected by the conflict. Even those children who have not been abused themselves have witnessed acts of violence. The psychological scars are deep. A UNICEF study *(see page 17)* in October 1997 found that 90 per cent

---

[53] UNICEF, *The State of the World's Children 1998*, Table 4 on nutrition.

[54] This book focuses on violations that occur in the context of armed conflict and in police detention. This is not to minimise other violations against children, especially girls, in South Asia. For more details, see Amnesty International, *Children in South Asia – securing their rights*, April 1998.

[55] Amnesty International, *Afghanistan – Children traumatised by civil war*, April 1998.

of children in Kabul had believed that they would die during the conflict. Two thirds had seen dead bodies or parts of dead bodies. Most of the children suffered from nightmares, anxiety and concentration problems. Almost all the children interviewed felt sometimes or often that life was not worth living.[56]

The legacy of landmines is an especially acute problem in Afghanistan. Up to ten million unexploded devices are thought to be scattered across the country.[57] One million mines are believed to be in the capital city Kabul. According to the Mine Clearance Planning Agency, more than 30 per cent of mine victims are children under the age of 12. Every day, seven children are wounded by mines. Most of them die as their small bodies cannot stand mine explosions. Many who survive the initial blast die later because of a lack of medical facilities.[58]

Several of the warring factions in South Asia exploit the vulnerability of children and recruit them as soldiers. Many children 'volunteer' because they are destitute or have lost their families. Others are forcibly recruited, either directly or, in the case of Afghanistan and Pakistan, through religious schools known as *madrases,* often without the consent of their parents (*see page 59*).

Several juveniles have been 'disappeared' after being detained in Jammu and Kashmir, in northwest India. Fourteen-year-old Nazir Ahmad Gojar was grazing cattle in Gojar Pathi Malagam, Bandipora, district Baramula, when army personnel picked him up along with two other men during a search operation on 26 January 1992. The arrest was witnessed by neighbours. One of those arrested was released after five months. He said that they had been beaten before being brought to a nearby army camp and transferred to another camp. Nazir Ahmad Gojar was not seen again after the three were separated on around 29 January 1992.

A judicial inquiry concluded in May 1996 that '...the failure of the army of not disclosing the whereabouts of missing individual Nazir Gojar so far suggests with force that it is a clear case of custodial disappearance of the missing individual... about whom the presumption of death during custody can be drawn'. No-one has been prosecuted for his death.[59]

---

[56] Amnesty International, *Children in South Asia – securing their rights,* April 1998.
[57] *Hidden Killers*, US State Department report, 1993, cited in *Children at War,* Save the Children Fund, 1994.
[58] Amnesty International, *Children in South Asia – securing their rights,* April 1998.

Many young girls have suffered sexual harassment or rape by security forces in Jammu and Kashmir. In the night of 22-23 April 1997, during a raid of Wavoosa village near Srinigar, at least four security personnel raped 14-year-old Gulshan, her 15-year-old sister Kulsuma and her 16-year-old sister Rifat. In a neighbouring house they raped 17-year-old Naza and at least three adult women. Army and civilian authorities made inquiries into the incident but no steps appear to have been made to bring those responsible to justice.[60]

In the northeast Indian state of Manipur, Indian army soldiers often suspect teenagers of being members or supporters of the armed opposition. On the evening of 12 February 1998, Yumlembam Sandamacha was taken from his home by members of the 17th Rajputana Rifles. Two other boys were taken from the same village. All three were beaten. Yumlembam was subjected to severe torture. The next day the two other boys were released into police custody. Yumlembam 'disappeared' and the army denied that he had ever been detained.

Children have also been the silent witnesses to terrifying violations in Manipur. On 4 April 1998, a woman – Laishram Ningol Ningthoujam Ongbi Pramo Devi – was raped in Keirenphabi village in Manipur. Her four-year-old son was reportedly held with a gun to his head by army personnel just outside the house in which she was being raped. Similarly, an eight-year-old boy suffering from polio was forced to witness the rape of his mother, Ahanjaobi Devi, in the outskirts of Imphal in August 1996.[61]

Street children and 'justice'

'Children in many countries face the wrath of the law for the "crimes" of being poor, neglected or abused. Regardless of the reasons for their offences, young people are entitled to fair treatment at the hands of juvenile justice systems that are designed to aid youngsters' return to productive society as quickly as possible.'

Lisbet Palme, *No age of innocence: Justice for children,* The Progress of Nations, United Nations Children's Fund (UNICEF) 1997.

---

[59] Amnesty International, *Children in South Asia – securing their rights,* April 1998.
[60] Amnesty International, *Children in South Asia...,* April 1998.
[61] Amnesty International, *India – Manipur: The silencing of youth,* May 1998.

Previous page: **Family living in El Monton rubbish dump, Rimac, Lima Peru**

© Carlos Reyes-Manzo

Justice systems the world over violate the basic human rights of children who come into contact with the law. Children are tortured and ill-treated in police custody. They are held in prisons in inhuman and degrading conditions. They are denied due process which should guarantee them fair trials. They are given sentences which disregard the key principles of juvenile justice – rehabilitation, and the primacy of the well-being of the child.

Most children who come into conflict with the law do so for minor, non-violent offences and in some cases their only 'crime' is that they are poor, homeless and disadvantaged. Factors such as poverty, ethnicity and gender compound children's vulnerability to abuse at the hands of the law.[62] Children forced to live on the streets are particularly vulnerable to arbitrary arrest and ill-treatment. Their poverty brings them into the path of the law: Some are arrested under laws which make destitution, vagrancy and begging criminal offences. Others are detained and ill-treated simply because they are easy prey.

The children who end up living on Colombia's notoriously violent urban streets face the threat of what is euphemistically called 'social cleansing'. Shadowy death squads, said to comprise off-duty police officers, run 'cleansing' operations – killing people they consider undesirable. Dumped bodies frequently bear marks of torture. Many are never identified.[63]

The children who survive through petty crime and begging or who end up in Colombia's street gangs, are targeted along with other 'undesirables' like vagrants, drug addicts and gay men. Posters have been stuck up in the capital Bogotá, inviting 'delinquents' to come to their own funerals.

In Rio de Janeiro, street children were murdered so often that the state assembly set up a parliamentary commission to investigate the killings. It found that in Rio de Janeiro State alone, 427 children and adolescents were murdered in 1990, most of them by death squads which in many cases involved off-duty police officers hired by local shop keepers to 'clean up' the area from alleged criminals and petty thieves.[64]

---

[62] Amnesty International, *'The best interests of the child' – Human Rights and the juvenile justice system*, October 1998.

[63] Amnesty International, *Colombia: Children and minors – victims of political violence*, June 1994.

[64] Amnesty International, *Brazil – Impunity and the law: the Killing of Street Children in Rio de Janeiro State*, March 1992.

Two years later, in July 1993, a gang of hooded men opened fire on a group of over 50 street children sleeping rough near the Candelária Church, one of Rio de Janeiro city's most prominent landmarks. Seven children and one adult were killed. The massacre provoked an international outcry and an official investigation led quickly to the prosecution of three military police officers and a civilian for the murders. Further investigations implicated five other military policemen in the massacre. In April 1996, in the first trial in the case, military policeman Marcos Vinícius Borges Emanuel, 29, was sentenced to a total of 309 years imprisonment for his part in the massacre. At a retrial in June 1996, the sentence was reduced to 89 years.[65] Five years after the Candelária massacre, on 25 August 1998, Marcos Aurelio Dias de Alcantara was convicted of killing eight street children and sentenced to 204 years in prison. In June 1998, the Rio state legislative assembly suspended promotions and pay bonuses based on 'bravery', which reportedly had led to a 100 per cent increase in the number of civilian deaths resulting from police actions.

Despite these convictions, the Brazilian authorities have not effectively investigated other extrajudicial executions. Nor have they provided adequate protection for witnesses to such killings, including the Candelária massacre. Only one witness to the massacre had the full protection of the federal authorities, following a second attempt on his life in December 1994.

Some 5,000 children live on the streets of Guatemala City, some, reportedly are orphans whose parents were killed by the Guatemalan army in the civil conflict which shook the country over a period of more than three decades. In a country of 10 million people, tens of thousands of mainly indigenous people were killed in the army's counter-insurgency campaigns against left-wing guerrillas. Around one million fled their homes; hundreds of thousands crossed the border into Mexico. The scale of the murders was such that for several years, the main human rights reporting in Guatemala came from organisations of widows.

Casa Alianza, an organisation which has provided food and medical assistance to street children since the early 1980s, has documented a staggering level of abuse against these children. Between 1990 and 1996, 280 allegations of extrajudicial killing, torture, ill-treatment,

---

[65] Amnesty International, *Brazil – The Candelária trial: a small wedge in the fortress of impunity*, July 1996.

intimidation, illegal arrest, threats, injuries and abduction against street children have been reported. Official investigations are rare. While criminal gangs have reportedly been responsible in some incidents, *Casa Alianza* believes there is strong evidence of the involvement of members of the security forces in at least 180 of these cases.

In many cases, private security officers, whose number has proliferated in Guatemala in recent years, have been responsible. On 24 September 1994, Rubén García González, 14, Daniel Rosales, 10 and Víctor Manuel García, 12, were trying to sleep in Zone 4 of Guatemala City when a woman nearby began screaming. Two private security men from the *Los Vigilantes* company approached the children and opened fire. Daniel Rosales died instantly. Rubén García died later in hospital. This case is one of the extremely rare cases in Guatemala to lead to a prosecution. On 6 June 1996, the two men were sentenced to 30 years imprisonment. In November 1996, an appeal resulted in one having his sentence reduced to 10 years' imprisonment. The other was acquitted.[66]

Street children in other parts of the world face similarly brutal treatment at the hands of the police. In India, Rajesh, a 14-year-old ragpicker, was dragged into a jeep by several policemen in Trivandrum, Kerala state, in May 1996. No reasons were given for his arrest. Police officers reportedly pierced his finger nails with pins, banged his head against the wall, forced him to sit on an imaginary chair for long periods, and beat the soles of his feet. The police denied that Rajesh was in their custody and transferred him between police stations to conceal his whereabouts. When he was finally released on bail on 10 June, he needed hospital treatment for injuries sustained while in police custody. Amnesty International knows of no inquiry into Rajesh's illegal detention and torture.

Girls without power

The particular vulnerabilities of girls and women are exploited by the forces supposed to protect them. Police in Bangladesh frequently take young girls into 'safe custody' during investigations into allegations of rape. Many girls in 'safe custody' are then raped and sexually abused. Yasmin Akhter, 14, was raped and killed by three police officers in

[66] Amnesty International, *Guatemala – State of Impunity*, 24 April 1997. And also: *Guatemala – Children in fear: Street children and street educators continue to be targeted*, May 1992.

August 1995. She was picked up by the police in their patrol car on the pretext of giving her a lift home to her mother's house in Dinajpur. They later dumped her body by the roadside. The police tried to cover up the crime by claiming Yasmin was a prostitute and died jumping out of the moving van. The policemen were eventually tried and found guilty in 1997.[67]

Conclusions

The violation of children's human rights occurs across the globe. The perpetrators often act with impunity and are rarely called to account (*see Chapter 5*). The numbers of victims stretch into the millions. These violations are not accidental. The term 'collateral damage' was designed to disguise the fact that civilian casualties are 'factored in' to modern warfare.

But such callous calculations are also the source of hope. Children are caught up in armed conflicts as a result of adult (usually male) decisions. Armies do not *have to* indiscriminately shell civilian areas. Soldiers do not *have to* commit rape or other atrocities against girls who belong to the wrong ethnic group or whose parents hold the 'wrong' political views. Armies are disciplined human structures. Obeying orders is central to military discipline. Military leaders can issue orders that civilians must not be targeted or mistreated, and that offenders will be punished.

Protection of children in armed conflicts is a question of political will. Soldiers act with impunity when nothing holds them to account. But put in place the right orders, the right system of discipline and the right value on the lives and welfare of children and this can change.

The success of the campaign to ban anti-personnel mines was achieved by stigmatising the use of an established military tactic on the grounds of its cruelty to society. What is needed now to protect children is a crusade to stigmatise any targeting of children in armed conflicts – in declared wars or otherwise.

---

[67] Amnesty International, *'The best interests of the child' – Human rights and the juvenile justice system*, October 1998.

3

Child soldiers

Rachel Brett

'I would like to give you a message. Please do your best to tell the world what is happening to us, the children. So that other children don't have to pass through this violence.'

The 15-year-old girl who ended an interview to Amnesty International with this plea was forcibly abducted at night from her home ... by the Lord's Resistance Army (LRA), an armed opposition movement fighting the Ugandan Government. She was made to kill a boy who tried to escape. She witnessed another boy being hacked to death for not raising the alarm when a friend ran away. She was beaten when she dropped a water container and ran for cover under gunfire. She received 35 days of military training and was sent to fight... the government army.[68]

Recruiting children, by force or persuasion, making them kill and commit other atrocities so as to brutalise them and make it hard for them to return to their communities, is by no means unique to the LRA even if its systematic abduction of large numbers of child recruits – an estimated 5,000 to 8,000 children since 1995[69] – is exceptional.

At least 300,000 under-18s are currently engaged in active combat. Thousands more are in armed forces which could be sent into combat at any time.[70] Precise figures are impossible to calculate. The overall strength of many of the armed groups which use child soldiers is a matter of speculation; they themselves are little concerned to keep accurate records of the ages of their personnel – and, insofar as they

---

[68] Amnesty International: *Uganda: 'Breaking God's commands': the destruction of childhood by the Lord's Resistance Army.* 18 September 1997, AI Index: AFR 59/01/97.
[69] Statement by Carol Bellamy, Executive Director of the United Nations Children's Fund (UNICEF), CF/DOC/PR/1997/27, 3 July 1997.
[70] Rachel Brett and Margaret McCallin: *Children the Invisible Soldiers* (2nd edition, Radda Barnen, Stockholm, 1998).

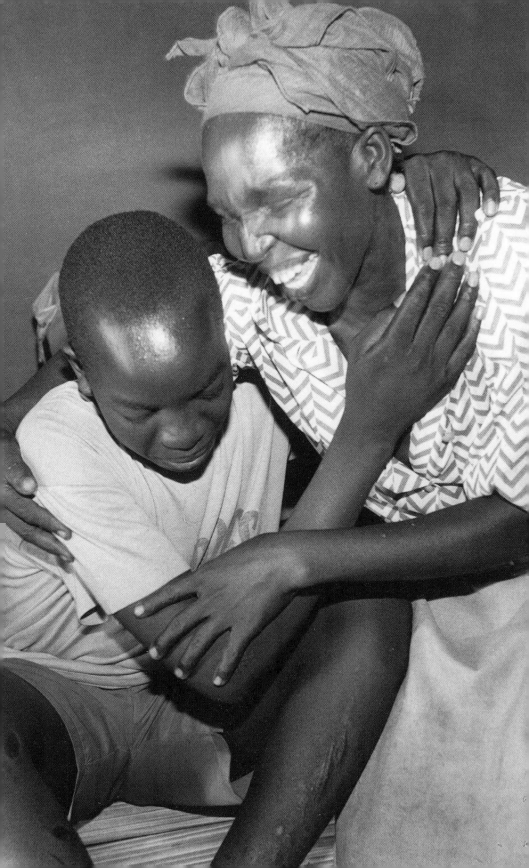

breach international law by using child soldiers, they have every incentive not to do so. In any case, child recruitment is subject to major fluctuations according to the ebb and flow of conflicts, and since the children themselves grow older: many of those initially recruited as children become adult soldiers or are demobilised as adults.

The majority of child soldiers are between the ages of 15 and 18 and therefore not illegal under current international law. Fifteen is the minimum age for recruitment and participation in hostilities specified in the Convention on the Rights of the Child, the 1977 Additional Protocols to the Geneva Conventions and the Statute of the International Criminal Court. However, many child soldiers are younger: numerous reports[71] have pointed to 10 as the watershed age at which a child can carry and operate a lightweight automatic weapon such as an AK-47, but the involvement of even younger children has been reported from many conflicts.[72]

All areas of the world where there are armed conflicts are affected.[73] This currently means that the largest number of child soldiers are in Africa and Asia, but no region is free from the problem. Many Western countries are among those who recruit under-18s (albeit voluntarily and with parental consent) into their regular armed forces – the UK not only recruits 16-year-olds but routinely deploys under-18s. Obviously there are differences of degree: the age of the children concerned, whether they experience combat, and how well regulated and disciplined are the forces which employ them. Nevertheless the experiences of child soldiers, the effects on the children concerned, and the resultant problems are similar in all cultural contexts.

Who become child soldiers?

'As armed conflict in Sierra Leone has intensified in recent years, the social fabric of the country has unraveled, and children have increasingly seen their rights erode. Many children have lost or been separated from their parents in the fighting, do not have

---

[71] Most recently Human Rights Watch, *Proxy Targets, Civilians in the War in Burundi*, March 1998.

[72] See Rachel Brett and Margaret McCallin, *Children the Invisible Soldiers*, 2nd edition, Rädda Barnen, Stockholm, 1998; Amnesty International: *Children in South Asia*. April 1998, AI Index: ASA 04/01/98; Human Rights Watch: *Sierra Leone, Sowing Terror, Atrocities against Civilians in Sierra Leone*. July 1998, Vol.10, No.3(A).

[73] See Rädda Barnen, *Children in current or recent armed conflicts*, Stockholm, September 1998.

Traumatised ex-child soldier reunited with his mother. Uganda 1997.

© Stuart Freedman

enough to eat and do not have schools and other basic structure in place to meet their needs. They are particularly vulnerable to forced recruitment ...'[74]

'There are areas where children beg insistently to join the guerrillas, but there are also situations in which their very own mothers, who are desperate, take their children to the guerrillas because their families live in misery.'[75]

In almost all situations, the same groups of children are most likely to become child soldiers, whether they are recruited by the government or by an armed group, and whether compelled to join or volunteering. These are:
• children separated from their families, without families or with disrupted family backgrounds, eg orphans, refugee/displaced, street children, single-parent families, step-children;
• children with little or no education, or with no access to education;
• children from the most marginalised sectors of society and the lowest socio-economic groups;
• children from the war zones.

With the exception of the final category this applies equally to conflict situations and to 'peacetime' recruitment. Even where conscription applies, it is the better-educated, better-connected youngsters who are most likely to contrive exemption. Where there is a volunteer force, it is those with the minimum length of compulsory education who might otherwise face unemployment (UK) or those from disadvantaged minorities (blacks in the USA), who are disproportionately attracted to the armed forces while still minors.

Why child soldiers?

It is not new for children to become embroiled in warfare. However two developments in recent decades have been instrumental in producing the child soldier as a widespread modern phenomenon. The first has been the development of lightweight automatic weapons. An AK-47 or M16 makes a 10 or 12-year-old boy (or girl) an effective instrument of destruction. The second has been the shift towards

[74] Human Rights Watch: *Sierra Leone, Sowing Terror, Atrocities against Civilians in Sierra Leone*, July 1998, Vol.10, No.3(A).
[75] Human Rights Watch, *War Without Quarter: Colombia and International Humanitarian Law* (October 1998)

conflicts which pitch government armies not primarily against the armed forces of another state, but against a variety of armed opposition groups, in which fixed battle lines are the exception, the fight is usually carried out amid the civilian population which is itself frequently the target. Today it is not a question of teenage boys looking for adventure, but of children of both sexes willingly or unwillingly taking up arms in fights raging about their homes.

> *'We were leaving school at the end of the day and the SLORC (Burmese government) soldiers surrounded the school. I was in the 7th Standard then and we were writing our examinations. We'd just finished one or two subjects that afternoon. There were 40 or 50 of us all leaving together, and we were all arrested. We were all 15, 16, 17 years old... We were students, we looked like students, because we were all wearing our white shirts and green longyis. Our teachers all ran away in fear... We were all terrified, but we couldn't even call out to them to let us go and that we were under 18, because we were so scared... Our parents had no idea what happened to us. They weren't told anything and neither were we. Some people had money to pay off the SLORC officers, but most couldn't.'*[76]

Former child soldier Zaw Gyi (*pseudonym*)

Many child soldiers are recruited by force. Legislation may provide for compulsory military service, and may set an age limit of 18, but inefficiency, corruption, or structural inadequacies (for example the lack of a functioning system of birth registration) distort the reality. Many armies resort to the press gang. Random sweeps are made, usually in public places, but sometimes from house to house; young men who appear to be of military age – and frequently considerably lower – are seized, and only sometimes is there any opportunity for those who are not eligible for military service to prove this and obtain their release. Nor are governments alone in filling their ranks in this manner. A number of armed opposition groups have claimed to enforce a form of conscription on their client populations; others rely on abductions.

---

[76] Quoted in Images Asia, *No Childhood at All: Child Soldiers in Burma*, Chiangmai, Thailand, revised edition June 1997.

'I had gone to the garden to collect tomatoes at around eight or nine in the morning. Suddenly, I was surrounded by about 50 rebels. ...They arrested me and started beating me terribly. They wanted me to walk them to my home but I was refusing. Finally, I walked them to my home. We went there and collected my clothes. There, they killed my mother. They made me go, leaving behind my little brother and two little sisters. They are still very young. I was trying to explain to them that I could not leave behind the children because they were too young to fend for themselves. I was resisting. Then they started beating me until I became unconscious.'

B, a 14-year-old girl[77]

In July 1997 the father of 13-year-old Maroof Ahmad Awan filed a petition in the Sindh High Court in Karachi, Pakistan, accusing the principal of the local *Jamia Islamia* of sending his son to fight in Afghanistan without consulting the parents.... 'I handed him over to the school to learn the Qu'ran, not to handle guns. He's too young to fight in a war,' said his father. Maroof had joined the school in early May and was missing for several weeks until the school authorities admitted that he had left, supposedly of his own volition, to fight in Afghanistan.... A month later [he] returned, saying, 'I was persuaded to go to Afghanistan by the nazim of the school'. Some 600 other juveniles were reportedly taken in buses to Afghanistan on the same day.[78]

Refugee children are particularly at risk, and not only those who remain close to the war zone. In the summer of 1998 Kurdish children living in Sweden, invited to attend a summer camp, failed to return and are presumed to have been abducted by the PKK to fight in Turkey.[79]

However, many children join without being directly forced. For many, this is a simple case of survival – the soldiers have food or provide the guns which are a means of getting food. They may also provide shelter, protection and a substitute family for those who are orphaned, separated from families or alone for other reasons. Many children 'volunteer' because they or their families are destitute, or because they have lost their families and are homeless.[80]

---

[77] Amnesty International: *Uganda 'Breaking God's commands': the destruction of childhood by the Lord's Resistance Army* 18 September 1997, AI Index: AFR 59/01/97.
[78] Amnesty International: *Children in South Asia* April 1998, AI Index: ASA 04/01/98.
[79] Radda Barnen, *Children of War*, No. 3/98, Stockholm, September 1998

'I joined Kabila's army at the age of 13 because our house had been pillaged and my parents had left. Finding myself alone, I chose to become a soldier.'[81]

'I voluntarily joined the (government) soldiers, because there was no other means of food.'

Government soldier, age 14[82]

Others are attracted by the power and prestige attached to a military uniform, and some take sides in the war out of a conviction which is often a result of personal experience or social conditioning. Experience of ill-treatment and atrocities by government armed forces is the single major factor which makes children volunteer for opposition groups.

In many cases, minors are recruited when the supply of adults is inadequate for the manpower needs of the force concerned. Sometimes recruiters disregard the minimum age they are supposed to apply, if any, even when military commanders are less happy with very young recruits. As an internal armed conflict continues, government forces tend to recruit progressively younger people, both to meet their manpower needs and to deprive the opposition of potential fighters. Conversely, this 'pre-emptive recruitment' often encourages youths to join the opposition and escape service in the government army, creating a vicious circle, with an ever downward pressure on the age of involvement.

There are instances where children are explicitly preferred. They are seen as more malleable, less likely to question orders, or having fewer compunctions about committing atrocities:

'It appears that those in command believe that child soldiers are less likely to question orders from adults and are more likely to be fearless, as they do not appreciate the dangers they face.'[83]

'The kadogo (boy soldiers) make very good soldiers because they

---

[80] Amnesty International: *Children in South Asia* April 1998, AI Index: ASA 04/01/98.
[81] Testimony of a child soldier in the Democratic Republic of Congo, reported by Agence France Presse on 8 October 1998 *(translated)*.
[82] Women's Commission for Refugee Women and Children, *The Children's War, Towards Peace in Sierra Leone* June 1997.

don't worry about anything. They obey orders; they are not concerned about getting back to their wife or family. And they don't know fear, either.[84]

'*The younger the youth is, the better. The lads are more daring, they have more bravery in warfare. And although they are hardly given any kind of responsibility, what they are charged with they do much better.*'[85]

'*Young boys are targeted in part because their captors consider them to be less afraid to fight; they likely do not have children or wives to consider in risking their lives. They are readily manipulated because they are vulnerable and without protection.*'[86]

The attraction may not be purely military: 'The Lord's Resistance Army (LRA) rebels seem to target children aged 11 and above. There is no minimum recruitment age for the girls.... Any girl that has breasts beginning to emerge would be considered ripe for handing over to a man as a wife. With the increase of HIV/AIDS in Uganda, the rebels hoped that the younger girls would be virgins and therefore not likely to carry HIV.'[87]

How child soldiers are treated

'For all personnel under the age of 18, the Australian Defence Force assumes the responsibilities of 'in loco parentis'. These responsibilities include the provision of suitable accommodation, restriction of their social and leave activities. Recreational facilities are provided in an environment free from alcohol use. Their progress is regularly monitored by supervisory staff and there is ready access to chaplains, psychologists and other support staff. Apart from these provisions, they undergo the same training as their older colleagues. Because of this, their ability to cope with such training, especially their level of

---

[83] Amnesty International, *Children in South Asia* April 1998, AI Index: ASA 04/01/98.

[84] Congolese rebel officer, quoted by Agence France Press, 8/10/98.

[85] Guerrilla source quoted by Defensoria del Pueblo [Public Ombudsman's Office], Republic of Colombia, *Victimas de la violencia: El conflicto armado in Colombia y los menores de edad*, Bogota, May 1996.

[86] Human Rights Watch: *Sierra Leone, Sowing Terror, Atrocities against Civilians in Sierra Leone*. July 1998, Vol.10, No.3(A).

[87] World Vision, *Gulu: Children of War*, Milton Keynes, UK, December 1995.

maturity, is carefully assessed during the recruitment process and monitored during their subsequent training.'[88]

If we were seeking a model of good practice for the treatment of child soldiers, this would be a good start. It clearly recognises that the conditions and training deemed appropriate for recruits aged over 18 have different implications for a younger age group. However, those who make the most extensive use of child soldiers, and who, unlike Australia, deploy them on active service, do not usually display this level of solicitude for their physical and moral welfare. The training, if any, may be beyond the physical capacity of the children, and the military culture is typically unforgiving towards those who, often literally, fall by the wayside. In many, perhaps most, armed forces it can be accompanied by initiation rituals, themselves a source of human rights concern.[89] Military life often brings an introduction to abuses involving sex, alcohol and drugs. While the effects on an 18 or 19-year-old are hardly beneficial; at a younger age these experiences are in all respects immeasurably more harmful.

The general brutalisation of child recruits is often a deliberate policy, even in exceptional cases involving ritual cannibalism:[90] 'Once recruited, children are frequently exposed to brutal initiation ceremonies. They are made to endure horrific scenes in order to harden them to the violence they are expected to face or inflict on others, and in order to subordinate them to authority. In some cases, they are forced to commit atrocities against people known to them.'[91]

'Children are beaten, murdered and forced to become combatants. Girls are raped and used as sexual slaves by more senior soldiers. But in addition, becoming an involuntary part of the LRA means being made to abuse others. The killers of attempted escapees, captured government soldiers and civilians are themselves abused children. They are being abused by being forced to commit human rights violations. This is deliberate. The children are often traumatized by what they have done and, believing that they are now outcasts, they

---

[88] Part of the response by the Director General Personnel Policy and Plans of the Australian Defence Force to enquiries by the author about recruitment of personnel aged under 18, 1/5/96.
[89] *Human rights of conscripts*, Council of Europe Parliamentary Assembly, Committee on Legal Affairs and Human Rights. Rapporteur: Mr Erik Jurgens, Netherlands, Socialist Group, Doc.7979, 3 June 1998.
[90] See Rachel Brett and Margaret McCallin: *Children the Invisible Soldiers*, 2nd edition, Rädda Barnen, Stockholm, 1998.
[91] Amnesty International: *Children in South Asia*. April 1998, AI Index: ASA 04/01/98.

become bound to the LRA.'[92] From diverse environments come tales of the intoxication or doping of child soldiers in preparation for battle.

'Drugging youths before raiding a village or entering combat became commonplace.'[93]

'To calm our nerves we used to drink gunpowder in milk. If you take it by itself it gives you a headache. With the gunpowder you stay energetic, longing for the troops to pass in front of you so that you can kill them.'[94]

'...they ground 5 [tranquilliser] tablets and mixed them with army rum and gave them to 30 porters. The porters were sent to mined areas to sweep for mines. All of them died. Often the officers would mix 4 tablets with a bottle of rum for the soldiers or the porters, to increase their strength and courage, and dull their sensitivity and ability to feel pain.' '...some defectors told us that they were given whiskey before they went into battle. I don't know if they put something in the whiskey. But at Phalu, there were a lot of boys rushing the field, screaming like banshees when they rushed the barbed wire. It seemed like they thought they were immortal or impervious or something'[95]

Sometimes, child soldiers are singled out for special treatment or duties. Their small size and agility make them 'ideally suited' for planting and detecting landmines, or recovering weapons and other booty from corpses in 'no man's land'. Their apparent innocence makes them ideal for espionage or as decoys – an apparently abandoned small child may tempt soldiers of one faction into an ambush set by another. They are often sent out to commit atrocities, being regarded as more malleable in this respect.

A child does not have to be armed to be a soldier. The very smallest

[92] Amnesty International: *Uganda 'Breaking God's commands': the destruction of childhood by the Lord's Resistance Army.* 18 September 1997, AI Index: AFR 59/01/97.

[93] Women's Commission for Refugee Women and Children: *The Children's War, Towards Peace in Sierra Leone.* June 1997.

[94] Former child soldier Juan Camilo (pseudonym) quoted by Defensoria del Pueblo [Public Ombudsman's Office], Republic of Colombia, *Victimas de la violencia: El conflicto armado in Colombia y los menores de edad*, Bogota, May 1996.

[95] Two testimonies quoted by Images Asia, *No Childhood at All: Child Soldiers in Burma*, Chiangmai, Thailand, revised edition June 1997.

may be adopted as orphans by military units and used as mascots; those slightly older may find themselves acting as the household servants of officers, graduating as they grow to taking messages, standing watch, and portering. Even so, 'In combat situations, military commanders may be tempted to make use of all the resources at their disposal, including under-age troops. As military personnel, those under eighteen are considered combatants, and may be the objects of attack, even without being placed in combat situations.'[96] In armed opposition groups, children may be born and grow up within guerrilla camps, and therefore be treated as targets by government forces, but initially such children are no more soldiers than are the civilian families of regular military personnel. In such a context, however, life is dominated by the conditions of armed struggle, and it takes a very determined and principled command structure to prevent youngsters from taking an active role from an early age and bearing weapons as soon as they are physically capable.

The trauma of soldiering

'Fifteen-year-old Raja (pseudonym) went to the Teaching Hospital in Jaffna, Sri Lanka, complaining of insomnia, aggressive outbursts and irrational abnormal behaviour in late 1994. He had joined the LTTE at the age of 11 and underwent extensive training. ... When recounting one attack, he described how he had held a child by the legs and bashed its head against a wall and how he enjoyed hearing the mother's screaming.'[97]

'The demobilisation, rehabilitation and reintegration of these children will ultimately present an enormous challenge to all those involved in healing the wounds of war and building a future...'[98]

Those involved in demobilisation programmes for child soldiers are often struck by the acute psychological trauma and difficulties of adjustment these children display. Separated during their formative years from family and an environment which might nourish them, they

---

[96] Human Rights Watch, *War Without Quarter: Colombia and International Humanitarian Law* (October 1998).
[97] Amnesty International, *Children in South Asia*, April 1998.

Literacy, and rights, for former boy soldier in rehabilitation in Liberia. 1997.

© Jenny Matthews

bear the scars of the treatment they have received, of the 'battlefield' experiences they have survived, and often of the atrocities they have been led to commit – atrocities which may be remembered, too, by the families of the victims – a further impediment to the reintegration of former child soldiers in civilian life.

It is a lucky child who carries forward only psychological scars. Many do not survive to be demobilised. Death is an occupational hazard for all soldiers, but 'there are frequently higher casualty rates among children due to their inexperience, and lack of training. Because of their size and agility children may be sent on particularly hazardous assignments'.[99] Furthermore, they are less valuable to the forces which deploy them than are mature, experienced soldiers, and therefore when injured they may be treated as dispensable:

> '... if the soldiers were badly wounded, they just killed them. If they were only slightly wounded and could follow us, they let them

[98] Human Rights Watch, *Sierra Leone, Sowing Terror, Atrocities against Civilians in Sierra Leone*. July 1998, Vol.10, No.3(A).

[99] Amnesty International, *Old enough to kill but too young to vote*. January 1998, AI Index: IOR 51/01/98.

come. But if they can't follow, even when they're not seriously injured, they kill them. Sometimes the officers kill the men themselves, and sometimes they just leave them there.'[100]

Children who attempt to escape are frequently put to death. Capital punishment is often imposed for other offences, in violation of human rights and international humanitarian law. On 28 March this year a 15-year-old member of the presidential guard in the Democratic Republic of Congo was sentenced to death by a military tribunal:

'Muderwa was convicted of killing a member of a Red Cross football team...the killing followed a dispute between Muderwa and his fellow soldiers who wanted to play football and the Red Cross football team who wanted them to leave because they had booked the pitch. The hearing of the Cour d'ordre militaire, military order court, took place at the side of the pitch immediately after the event, giving Muderwa's lawyer no time to prepare the defence.'[101]

Those who survive battle may suffer disproportionately from injuries when compared with adult soldiers. In part this stems from their distinctive duties, for instance those used in minefields have a high incidence of loss of limbs and loss of sight. In all circumstances injuries, and their consequences, can be worse as a result of incomplete physical development. Children are in greater danger than adults of losing their hearing through exposure to gunfire. Their growth may be stunted or distorted as a result of being forced to bear weights beyond their physical capacity.

Child soldiers are particularly exposed to physical hardship, disease and malnutrition. In particular because of the sexual demands to which they are frequently subjected, demobilised child soldiers of both sexes display exceptionally high rates of HIV/AIDS infection. Girls who become pregnant face either abortion or childbirth in insanitary conditions. Many of the children suffer from drug or alcohol abuse.

In short, many former child soldiers bear disabilities which form a lasting burden and have repercussions on their ability to re-reintegrate into civilian society by pursuing education and training or finding employment.

---

[100] Former child soldier Maung Hla Tint (pseudonym) quoted in Images Asia, *No Childhood at All: Child Soldiers in Burma*, Chiangmai, Thailand, revised edition June 1997.

[101] Amnesty International Urgent Action 24/98, 30/3/98 (AI Index AFR 62/13/98).

At the same time, all children who have been engaging in armed conflict at an age when they might have been expected to be in education carry a double burden. On the one hand they lack the training which would equip them for a constructive role in civil society, on the other they have learned to use a gun, and been indoctrinated into violent lifestyle and using force to achieve their objectives. These disadvantages are not readily remedied. Demobilised soldiers are embarrassed to be shown to be functionally illiterate, are ashamed to be sent back to school like the little children they were before taking up arms, and their touchiness can reveal itself in violent and disruptive behaviour. Nor is it simply a matter of 'book learning'. Even in societies where formal education is not widespread, child soldiers can miss vital formative years in learning traditional methods of agriculture or basics of a craft. Many child soldiers will not be identified and planned for in the demobilisation because their existence becomes an embarrassment to their leaders, and so they are abandoned as war moves towards peace. Others are not identified as child soldiers because they are now adults, although the fact that they were recruited and served as children will leave them with many of the same problems as those who end their involvement while still children.

The implications of child soldiering are broader than the individual child's exposure to potential death. There are much wider physical, mental and emotional consequences for each child so involved, violating many of their human rights. Furthermore, once children start becoming involved, it puts all children in the conflict zone at risk of recruitment or suspicion of involvement, exposing them to other violations. The involvement of children, particularly when combined with the brutalisation and abusive practices associated with their recruitment, has implications for the way the conflicts are fought – and may indeed be a factor in prolonging them or increasing post-conflict violence and instability.

And there are far-reaching questions for the future of societies with large numbers of children and young adults who have missed out on education, have been indoctrinated into violence and may be suffering from physical and psychosocial problems, and who need to be reintegrated into a society whose structure, economic and educational base have been disrupted if not destroyed by the conflict.

4

Refugee children

Simon Russell

'The angel of the Lord appeareth to Joseph in a dream, saying,
Arise, and take the young child and his mother and flee into
Egypt, and be thou there until I bring thee word: for Herod will
seek the young child and destroy him. When he rose he took the
young child and his mother by night and departed into Egypt:
and was there until the death of Herod.'[102]

The flight of children from persecution is not a new phenomenon.
Perhaps the most famous reported case of a child being forced into
exile is the infant Jesus (*above*). The end of the Cold War has seen an
upsurge of forced displacement as a consequence of increased
instability throughout the world. The Office of the UN High
Commissioner for Refugees (UNHCR) states that the refugee
phenomenon has assumed new dimensions since the late 1980s. The
number of people who could be described as victims of forced
displacement has reached a staggering 50 million, with new areas of
the world affected by refugee flows. At the same time, the commitment
of the international community to the concept of asylum has
weakened considerably.[103]

Children have always been caught up in violent conflicts and
consequent refugee flows. However, as the history of this century
illustrates, children have also been targeted either by genocidal
governments or by authorities hostile to particular groups of children.
As a result, children have been forced into exile alone to reach areas of
safety. During the Nazi regime thousands of Jewish children were sent
to safety on 'Kindertransport'; during the genocide in Rwanda, over
100,000 unaccompanied children fled into neighbouring countries.

---

[102] Matthew, 2:13
[103] *The State of the World's Refugees 1997-1998*. UNHCR

The UNHCR lists over 22 million people around the world as being of concern. Of those, 13.2 million people are classed as refugees in the 'conventional' sense, meaning people who have left their own country to escape from persecution, armed conflict or violence. A further 4.85 million people are listed as internally displaced.[104]

A special vulnerability

The High Commissioner points out that, usually, more than half of any refugee population are children, and they are especially vulnerable[105]. Not all of those children will be unaccompanied, indeed the majority of them will be with their mothers. But this does not make the refugee child any less vulnerable. Women refugees are also vulnerable; in addition to the basic needs of all refugees to be protected against attack or forced return to the country of origin, to have access to food, clothing, shelter, medical care and to have access to protection, women refugees also need protection against, sexual and physical abuse and exploitation, and sexual discrimination in the delivery of services.[106]

Nyorovai Whande, coordinator for women and children at

[104] op cit *UNHCR, The State of the World's Refugees 1997-1998.*
[105] *Refugee children: Guidelines on protection and care.* UNHCR, 1994
[106] *Guidelines on the protection of refugee women.* UNHCR, 1991

Refugee child from Kosovo in emergency accommodation in Brent, north London. 1998.

© Howard Davies

UNHCR, points out that any discussion of the protection of refugee children must include the protection needs of women who are, overwhelmingly, the care-givers.[107] Refugee children are, therefore, peculiarly vulnerable: they are vulnerable not only as refugees, but also as children who, in the majority of cases, are dependent upon their mothers who, as women refugees, are themselves vulnerable. This vulnerability leaves children open to violence, to disruption of community and social structures and to shortage of basic resources which affects physical and psycho-social development.[108] At the present time, the effects of displacement are graphically illustrated by the emergency in southern Sudan, where thousands of displaced mothers and children are at risk of malnutrition and even death by starvation.[109]

Unaccompanied refugee children are in an especially difficult position, without even a nominal carer to ensure survival. Unaccompanied children are defined as *'those who are separated from both parents and are not being cared for by an adult who, by law or custom, is responsible to do so'*.[110]

---

[107] *General issues relating to refugee children*, in *Justice for children*. Stewart Asquith & Malcolm Hill, eds. 1994.

[108] op cit, UNHCR *State of World's Refugees 1997-1998*

[109] See, for example, coverage of the situation in Sudan by ITN, 8 September 1998

[110] op cit, UNHCR *Refugee children: guidelines on protection and care,* 1994.

Ms Graça Machel's report to the UN on the impact of armed conflict on children. Her final report eloquently put the vulnerability of children in flight:

> 'To flee from one's home is to experience a deep sense of loss, and the decision to flee is not taken lightly. Those who make this decision do so because they are in danger of being killed, tortured, forcibly recruited, raped, abducted or starved, among other reasons. They leave behind them assets and property, relatives, friends, familiar surroundings and established social networks. Although the decision to leave is normally taken by adults, even the youngest children recognise what is happening and can sense their parents' uncertainty and fear.

> 'During flight from the dangers of conflict, families and children continue to be exposed to multiple physical dangers. They are threatened by sudden attacks, shelling, snipers and landmines, and must often walk for days with only limited quantities of water and food. Under such circumstances, children become acutely undernourished and prone to illness, and they are the first to die. Girls in flight are even more vulnerable than usual to sexual abuse. Children forced to flee on their own to ensure their survival are also at heightened risk... Children are often separated from parents in the chaos of conflict, escape and displacement. Parents or other care-givers are the major source of a child's emotional and physical security and for this reason family separation can have a devastating social and psychological impact. Unaccompanied children are especially vulnerable and at risk of neglect, violence, military recruitment, sexual assault and other abuses...'[111]

In Kosovo on 30 July 1998, three doctors were called to the village of Ribane some 30km from Pristina. 102 civilians had reached this village from the forest of Berisha into which they had been driven from their homes by direct military attacks. These 102 persons were attempting to live in one house. All were women and children. Three of the children were suffering frequent seizures. Their medicines to prevent fits had been lost during displacement from their homes. There were two newborn babies who had been born in the forest and who were still wrapped in their mothers' shirts.

---

[111] op cit, UN, *Impact of armed conflict on children* report

While attending to a woman who had been severely wounded, a nine-year-old girl called Hana called to the doctors. She was not able to speak clearly due to emotion and would not look the doctors in the face. She made the following statement: 'I saw his brain in the grass and she (her mother) is lying to me (saying her father is still alive). If you give me some water to drink and some bread maybe I will tell you how they killed my father and my grandfather and put my home on fire. I can't go back there. We have slept three nights in the woods. We did not eat or drink. I'm cold. I'll never see my father anymore. I'll never have a home. I just want to die. My village doesn't exist anymore. My school is burned. My brother is missing. I want to die.'

Testimony collected by Child Advocacy International, 1998

The international framework

The special vulnerability of refugee children has been frequently the subject of international concern. It was in response to the plight of refugee children from the Balkans that Eglantyne Jebb, founder of the Save the Children Fund (SCF), submitted a draft Declaration on the Rights of the Child to the League of Nations in 1924.[112]

The undesirability of forcing children into a situation where they become unaccompanied is underlined by the provisions of Article 78(1) of Protocol I additional to the Geneva Conventions 1949, prohibiting the evacuation of children to a foreign country except for compelling reasons of health or safety, and the provisions of Article 4(3)(b) of Protocol II, calling for measures to be taken to re-unite children separated by conflict from their families. These provisions echo concerns throughout the Geneva Conventions and Protocols about children in war and the need to re-unite them with families if separated. The importance of family unity is a constant theme, not only in humanitarian law, but also in human rights law and international standards on the treatment of refugees.

In 1987 the Executive Committee of the High Commissioner's Programme underlined what it called the special situation of unaccompanied children, including their needs as regards determination of their status, provision for their physical and emotional support and efforts to trace parents or relatives.[113] These Conclusions are not legally binding on States Parties to the 1951 Convention relating to the Status of Refugees[114] and the 1967 Protocol but are of persuasive authority. The 1987 Conclusion led the UNHCR

---

[112] *Children in Europe*. Sandy Ruxton, NCH Action for Children, 1996
[113] Conclusion No. 47 (XXXVIII) 1987, 38th Session
[114] 189 UNTS 150

to develop guidelines on refugee children which were revised in 1994.

Perhaps of more significance are the provisions concerning refugee children in the 1989 UN Convention on the Rights of the Child (CRC).[115] Article 22 states that:

'1. States Parties shall take appropriate measures to ensure that a child who is seeking refugee status or who is considered a refugee in accordance with applicable international or domestic law and procedures shall, whether unaccompanied or accompanied by his or her parents or by any other person, receive appropriate protection and humanitarian assistance in the enjoyment of applicable rights set forth in the present Convention and in other international human rights or humanitarian instruments to which the said States are Parties.'

Article 22 of the Convention is not, therefore, a stand-alone provision relating to refugee children but ensures that they are given the same rights as citizen children.

The question of refugee children was addressed again at the 1993 World Conference on Human Rights in Vienna. The Vienna Declaration and Programme of Action called for the strengthening of national and international mechanisms for the defence and protection of, *inter alia*, refugee and displaced children[116] and supported the Secretary-General's proposal to initiate a study into the means of improving the protection of children in armed conflicts (the Machel Study referred to above).[117]

The needs of refugee children
Identification

The Convention on the Rights of Child recognised that children not only have needs to be met but also rights to be respected. As the first priority in ensuring these rights are respected, the Machel study pointed out the enormous importance of identifying the child as unaccompanied and ensuring his or her survival and protection.[118] Identification of the child is considered so important that the details of what information must be recorded is part of international humanitarian law.[119] It is only when a child has been identified that his or her needs can be met and rights guaranteed.

---

[115] GA Res 44/25, annex, 44 UN GAOR Supp. (No.49) at 167, UN Doc A/44/49 (1989)
[116] Para.21
[117] Para.50
[118] Para.70
[119] Article 78(3) Protocol 1 additional to the Geneva Conventions of 1949

Relevant rights

For refugee children, UNHCR has characterised those rights in the Convention which affect refugee children the most as a triangle ensuring survival and development (guaranteed by Article 6 of the CRC).[120] The three rights identified by the UNHCR are the 'best interests' principle (Article 3), non-discrimination (Article 2), and participation (Article 12).

'Best interests' and non-discrimination

The 'best interests' principle and non-discrimination guarantee are clearly important in establishing a refugee child's right to protection and assistance. For example, in ratifying the Convention, the United Kingdom entered a wide-ranging reservation concerning immigration and asylum aimed at Articles 9 (concerning contact of a child with his or her parents) and 22 (concerning refugee children). However, given the open-ended nature of the reservation and the fact that it impacts upon the absolute obligations under Article 2 and 3 of the CRC there is some doubt as to whether the reservation does not seek to deny the 'object and purpose' of the Convention, which is to ensure the protection of all children, and is, therefore, disallowed.[121]

The UK's reservation to Article 22 is particularly invidious, given that Article 22 promotes the rehabilitation of victims of some of the severest crimes in the world. However, the 'catch-all' guarantees in Articles 2 and 3 are important in establishing that *all* children within the jurisdiction must be afforded the rights in the Convention and any reservation to Article 22 does not affect obligations under Articles 2 and 3.[122]

The right to participate in decisions

The right to participation in decision-making is an important corollary of the recognition that children are not just the objects of concern but also subjects of international law with recognised rights which have to be met. In determination of refugee status an interview is usually envisaged.[123] The question arises as to whether unaccompanied refugee

---

[120] op cit, UNHCR, State of the Word's Refugees 1997-1998.

[121] 1969 Vienna Convention on the Law of Treaties. See General Comment 24 of the UN Committee on Human Rights (52nd Session, 1994)

[122] The obligations of States towards aliens within the jurisdiction, including to obviate harm which may occur after removal is well-established. See, eg, *Soering v United Kingdom*

children should be subjected to an interview. Article 12 of the CRC
states that:

1. States Parties shall assure to the child who is capable of forming his or her own views
the right to express those views freely in all matters affecting the child, the views of the
child being given due weight in accordance with the age and maturity of the child.

2. For this purpose, the child shall in particular be provided the opportunity to be heard
in any judicial or administrative proceedings affecting the child, either directly, or through
a representative or an appropriate body, in a manner consistent with the procedural
rules of national law.[124]

Article 12 of the CRC is an attempt to give effect to the idea that the
child is an autonomous individual. It is consistent with Lord
Scarman's view in the *Gillick*[125] case that a child has a 'right to make his
own decisions when he reaches a sufficient understanding and
intelligence to be capable of making up his own mind on the matter
requiring decision'. It is important to note that States Parties have a
positive duty to help a child capable of *forming* views to express them
and not merely a passive obligation not to interfere in a right to
freedom of expression.

However, there is, of course, a great difference between consulting a
child and asking him or her to recount a story or to relate fears (in this
case, of being persecuted) but it cannot automatically be assumed that
the child should not tell his or her story. The important point made in
both Article 12 and by Lord Scarman is that whether the child makes his
or her own decision (or in this case, is asked to recount a possibly
traumatic story) depends upon what can be *loosely* called the maturity of
the child: maturity does not necessarily depend upon chronological age.

It may be useful to look at a case from the USA concerning age and
immigration.[126] In *Perez-Funez* the Californian District Court
disagreed[127] with the distinction made in the US *Immigration &
Nationality Act* of 1980 between those under and over 14. In the US
14 was taken as the age at which an alien child was deemed sufficiently
mature to engage in immigration proceedings, even without the
assistance of an adult. The court found that:

---

[123] Para.200, UNHCR Handbook
[124] Article 12, UN Convention on the Rights of the Child 1989
[125] *Gillick v West Norfolk and Wisbech Area Health Authority* 91986) AC 112
[126] Cf. *Perez-Funez v District Director*, INS 619 F Supp 656
[127] at 661-662

...unaccompanied children of tender years (the plaintiffs were between 11 and 16 years old) encounter a stressful situation in which they are forced to make critical decisions. Their interrogators are foreign and authoritarian. The environment is new and the culture completely different. The law is complex. The children generally are questioned separately. In short, it is obvious to the Court that the situation faced by unaccompanied minor aliens is inherently coercive...

It seems clear that whether a child should be interviewed or not about an asylum claim depends upon the maturity of the child and the availability of other sources of information. A personal interview should be a last resort and it is far preferable that the facts of an asylum claim are put forward through the offices of a competent lawyer. This would be consistent with the aim of Article 12 to ensure assistance is given to children in participating in decisions about themselves.

Detention of refugee children

The Machel study expressed concern that, 'one consequence of current policies is that a number of asylum-seekers, including children, are detained while their cases are considered..' The detention of asylum-seekers is restricted under Article 31 of the Refugee Convention which prohibits contracting states from imposing penalties on, or from restricting the movements of, refugees on account of illegal entry or presence. Conclusion 44 of the Executive Committee of the Programme of the United Nations High Commissioner for Refugees states that:

'...in view of the hardship which it involves, detention should normally be avoided. If necessary, detention should be resorted to only on grounds prescribed by law to verify identity; to determine the elements on which the claim to refugee status or asylum is based; to deal with cases where refugees or asylum-seekers have destroyed their travel documents in order to mislead the authorities of the State in which they intend to claim asylum; or to protect national security or public order'.

Many children are detained because they arrive in countries of asylum with false documents but there are a number of reasons why children

leave their home countries with false passports and why they often give false information to immigration officials in the country of asylum. In the majority of cases, exit and entry requirements have to be negotiated by agents, to whom the child is compelled to turn. These agents will often supply passports with false ages in order to obviate the need for parental consent to the exit of a child, especially in cases when the parents are missing. The agents also advise children to give false information in order to gain entry to a place of perceived safety. It is, of course, inevitable that a frightened child will follow the advice given and try and maintain false identities, very often to their own detriment.

Where no formal system of birth registration exists a child may not know his/her own true age. Where the child is an orphan or abandoned they may rely heavily upon the guidance of an agent who may find it easier to falsify a document than to prove a relationship with a child to the authorities in order to effect an exit.

The position of detained children in international law is stated in Article 37 of the Convention, thus:

> **'no child shall be deprived of his or her liberty unlawfully or arbitrarily'.**

The meaning of 'unlawful' does not solely depend upon whether detention is permitted under municipal law but is determined also by reference to international standards.[128] Where refugee children are detained there is a possible violation of Article 37 of the Convention as well as possible violation of Article 10(3) of the International Covenant on Civil and Political Rights and Article 14(4) of the same. The detention of refugee children, for whatever reason, flouts obligations under Article 22 of the Convention.

Detention of refugee children not only involves potential violations of international law but also a whole body of standards relating to the treatment of children and prisoners such as the UN Standard Minimum Rules on the Treatment of Prisoners, the UN Standard Minimum Rules on the Administration of Juvenile Justice (the *Beijing Rules*), and guidelines such as the UNHCR Handbook and UNHCR Guidelines on Refugee Children as well as UNHCR Executive Committee Resolutions.[129]

---

[128] See, eg *Chahal v United Kingdom*

Determining refugee status

Under the Refugee Convention a refugee is someone who *'owing to well-founded fear of being persecuted for reasons of race, religion, nationality, membership of a particular social group or political opinion'* is unable, or owing to such fear, is unwilling to return to his or her country of origin or former habitual residence.[130]

The Convention is facially neutral and makes no special provision for children. While the lack of such provision has not generated as much controversy as the debate over inclusion of gender-specific forms of persecution there have been several attempts, noted above, by UNHCR to focus the minds of governments of States Parties to the Refugee Convention on the special requirements of refugee children. Arguably, however, asylum-seeking refugee children are not well-served by the Convention or by the determination processes established to recognise refugee status.[131]

The Handbook recognises that children will, in particular, face difficulties in establishing a claim for asylum and calls for objective indications of risk to be looked at as well as a liberal application of the benefit of the doubt.[132] The Handbook also calls for the appointment of a guardian to promote decisions in the best interests of the child claimant. Aside from the difficulty in discharging the evidential burden, with which a guardian could assist, it is clear that a child will need a guardian also in order to safeguard his/her right to shelter, education and rehabilitation and to instruct counsel on the child's behalf.

The Refugee Convention engages the international community's obligations to those fleeing persecution in a limited way. Specifically, it restricts the definition of a refugee to those who flee persecution owing to a civil or political status. Some commentators have argued that the fourth limb, the 'membership of a particular social group' category is a catch-all.[133] However, the prevailing view is that the meaning of this phrase must be construed in the same way as the other grounds for refugee status.[134] Hence, those children who, for example, flee natural

---

[129] For an examination of the effects of detention on children see, eg *Slipping through the Cracks: Unaccompanied children detained by the US INS*. HRW/Children's Rights Project, 1997

[130] 1951 Convention relating to the Status of Refugees, Article 1 A(2).

[131] See, eg, *Through a Child's Eyes: protecting the most vulnerable asylum-seekers*. Jacqueline Bhabha and Wendy A Young. (1998) Interpreter Releases, Vol.75, No.21. June 1

[132] Paras.213-219 UNHCR Handbook

[133] Helton, A. *Persecution on account of membership in a social group as a basis for refugee status*. 1983. 15 Columbia HRLR 39.

disaster or civil war are not covered by the provisions of the Refugee Convention.

As this book makes clear, it should not be hard for child asylum claimants to establish that the persecution they fear is indeed based upon their civil or political status: it would be hard to deny, for example, that the victims of genocide are targeted because of their race or nationality. The facts show, however, that children are statistically less likely to be recognised as refugees than adult claimants. For example, in the United Kingdom claimants under 18 are seven times less likely to be recognised as refugees than those in the 25-29 age bracket.[135]

This is not just a problem of definition, although, as the experience of female claimants has shown, the mind-set of decision-makers is to see a refugee as a young male political activist. Indeed, asylum is often referred to as 'political asylum', disregarding the equally-important other grounds of protected status, with the notion of what constitutes the 'political' being equally narrow.[136] But it seems that, in addition, decision-makers do not recognise the specific forms of harm which children face or, more specifically, that the degree of harm faced cannot be measured in the same way as in an adult claimant's case. A simple example can illustrate this: it would be hard, although not impossible, to imagine that a claim for asylum by an adult on the grounds that he or she has no care-giver to return to would succeed. However, in a child's case such a scenario would constitute grounds for protection. The care-giver is responsible for the development and survival of the child and his or her absence would lay the child open to loss of fundamental rights, including the right to life.[137]

There have been some important steps to overcome the problems children face in establishing asylum claims but, to date, only by one State Party. The Canadian Immigration and Refugee Board has established guidelines on children[138], and the UNHCR followed suit with guidance based upon the 1994 Guidelines referred to above.[139]

---

[134] See, eg Hathaway, JC. *The law of refugeee status*. Butterworths, 1991.
[135] *Asylum Statistics UK 1997*. Home Office, 21 May 1998. Table 6.2.
[136] For a much fuller discussion of this problem see, eg *Women as asylum seekers: A legal handbook*. Heaven Crawley, Refugee Women's Legal Group, 1997.
[137] See, eg, the *dicta* of the UK Immigration Appeals Tribunal in *Sarjoh Jakitay v SSHD* unreported, (12658) IAT 15 November 1995.
[138] *Child refugee claimants: Procedural and evidentiary issues*. Ottawa, September 1996.
[139] UNHCR, *Guidelines on Policies and Procedures in dealing with Unaccompanied Children Seeking Asylum*. February 1997.

5

Children's rights in armed conflict

Dan Seymour

Children are the first victims of any war. Children are most vulnerable to injury and death. Sometimes they are specifically targeted as a way of terrorising their community. They are used as soldiers, sexually abused, tortured and exploited. Their opportunity to grow up in an environment that nurtures and promotes their development is taken away from them. They miss out on education, their health and nutrition suffer. The list goes on.

This goes on every day, in many places around the world. At the same time, children have rights to special protection and a case can be made for protection of children as a priority in time of armed conflict. There are many reasons for this. But two are overwhelming: children need special protection because they are vulnerable – both becase of the direct harm they sustain and the opportunities lost – and because children have a crucial role in peace-building and post-conflict reconstruction. Children also need to be recognised as potential actors in their own right.

The conduct of modern war, as shown in earlier chapters, now overwhelmingly affects civilians more than combatants. And the majority of civilians killed or wounded in time of war are children. Thus many issues of prevention of conflict, or at least modification of its conduct and the protection of civilians, are primarily children's issues. Children's rights are closely linked to one of the main obstacles to human rights protection in time of war; that of impunity. While wars and battlefields can be brutal, unthinking and chaotic places, it is also the case that many of the systematic and gross human rights violations of modern conflict were not carried out in the heat of the moment. They were planned and executed in a wholly deliberate fashion. They were premeditated. The genocide in Rwanda, the policies of torture and 'disappearance' of some conflicts in South America, the use of rape as a method of war in Bosnia, were not

accidents resulting from a rush of blood or temporary insanity.

A question of impunity

We are compelled to think 'never again', much as the drafters of the United Nations Charter did in 1945 in the wake of the Holocaust. Yet we must fear that indeed we will see these horrors again. As this book was being written, villages were being shelled in Kosovo in Yugoslavia, and whole communities forced to flee. It is useful to consider this example. Much of the killing and terror in Kosovo are under the control of the Yugoslav forces and Serb police. Some of the 'special' police brought in to deal with some ethnic Albanian dissent in Kosovo are believed to be veterans of the war in Bosnia, with a proven track record of brutality. In effect, they are people who carried out crimes in Bosnia for which they were never punished or even held accountable. The International Criminal Tribunal for the former Yugoslavia has had some success in bringing to justice those accused of war crimes and crimes against humanity in the former Yugoslavia, but many of those were only brought before the Tribunal in recent months.

Given this reality, it could be argued that the inability promptly to identify, prosecute and punish the war criminals of the former Yugoslavia has a direct causal link to the current death, injury and suffering taking place in Kosovo. Again, children are the first victims of war, and the same is no less true of Kosovo where, by November 1998, at least 150 ethnic Albanian children have been killed, primarily by shells or gunshot wounds.

The problem is generally described as one of impunity. The argument is that people commit grave human rights violations because they believe they will get away with it. And they appear to be right – they do get away with it in the vast majority of cases.

Wanted – a rule of law

The question then becomes one of how to tackle impunity. There are no easy answers, but the following appear to be prerequisites. First, there needs to be a rule of international law which is constant and which applies without distinction to all present and future conflicts, applying universal standards and with universal jurisdiction. Second, there needs to be a body capable of monitoring and enforcing those standards. Third, there needs to be the political will and the capacity made available to apprehend and try those suspected of breaching these standards.

There are now two *post facto* and ad hoc tribunals in place, one for the Former Yugoslavia and one for Rwanda, and there is a statute agreed for a permanent International Criminal Court (ICC), although the court is not yet active. Following considerable efforts by non-governmental organisations (NGOs), a number of provisions specific to the protection of children were included in this statute. Most notable of these was a provision which addressed the issue of child soldiers, enforcing the 15-year age limit specified in the UN Convention on the Rights of the Child (CRC) and the 1997 Additional Protocols to the Geneva Conventions of 1949. Broadly speaking, the statute makes it a war crime to use children under 15 as soldiers.

This provision greatly enhances existing standards. First of all, the crime of using children as soldiers becomes an 'individuated' crime. That is, unlike the the provisions of the CRC which impose an obligation on states which have chosen to be bound by them, the provisions of the statute make the actions of individuals directly punishable, regardless of whether those individuals have consented to the jurisdiction of the court. This is criminal law in the sense in which the lay person understands it; a set of non-negotiable rules which incur punishment when breached.

One implication arising from this individuated standard is that it formally relocates some of the blame for a child's actions when he or she has been used to fight. In Liberia many children were used to fight what was essentially a resource war between Liberian warlords. To instil obedience and an unhesitating capacity for brutality, these children were sometimes forced to commit atrocities against their own communities or families. In such contexts it is naive to expect these communities to welcome their children back after a conflict, yet it is at these times that children most need the support of their families. Where child soldiers are perceived solely as perpetrators and not victims, they often find that after a conflict they are singled out for revenge.

To recognise the culpability of the recruiter is to recognise that the child soldier is not solely responsible for his or her actions. It is worth considering how children from the world's wealthier countries might act if, at the age of, say, 12, they were abducted, routinely brutalised, desensitised to violence and put in a situation where killing was a way of life and the only way to get along.

A recent case from Uganda provides a good example. Two boys in their early teens were abducted by the Lord's Resistance Army (LRA) in Northern Uganda. They were made to fight and kill for their abductors. They were threatened with death if they did not comply. Like any child would, they did what they were told. Eventually, they were captured after a few years, still children, and put on trial as traitors. They faced a death sentence for what they had been forced to do. This is not to say that child soldiers should be absolved of all responsibility for their actions, but rather that it is not appropriate to hold them solely responsible.

An important feature of the provisions of the International Criminal Court is that these standards will apply as much to those fighting in non-governmental forces such as the LRA, the Sudan People's Liberation Army or Liberation Tigers of Tamil Eelam as to those fighting for the Ugandan, Sudanese or Sri Lankan government armed forces. Laudable and important as the efforts of those working currently at international level against the use of children as soldiers are, it is likely that the first prosecution by the International Criminal Court on grounds of being a child recruiter and user will be one of the main turning points in the struggle against this practice.

The key international human rights standard relating to children is the United Nations Convention on the Rights of the Child (CRC). The Convention was adopted by the United Nations General Assembly in 1989 and since then has been ratified by virtually every country in the world (with the exceptions of the USA and The collapsed state of Somalia). It is the most recent of the six central treaties of international human rights law, these being the treaties which set up international monitoring bodies.

The Convention is a very broad instrument, in many ways reiterating the provisions of the two International Covenants of 1966 but applying them specifically to children. There are a small number of additions, such as Article 12 which lays out a child's rights to have a say in decisions affecting him or her, or Article 22 which relates to disabled children. Generally speaking, the Convention is a comprehensive guide to the rights of children which most would recognise as basic ethical norms the treatment of children. It is possible to go through the 40 standard-setting articles of the Convention to determine which are violated at time of war. The answer is, usually, all of them.

With its near-universal ratification, and its comprehensive coverage of the range of children's rights, the Convention is a uniquely important set of standards for children. It establishes a normative framework for protection of and provision for children at an international level. It also, through its acceptance by diverse cultures around the world, makes a compelling case for the universality of these standards, and that they should be applied in the same way for all children whoever or wherever they might be.

Another effort currently underway is the attempt to create a new instrument of international law raising the minimum age for recruitment of children as soldiers and their participation in hostilities from 15 to 18. This would take the form of an Optional Protocol to the Convention – an optional add-on for states. The draft Protocol's primary purpose is to increase the protective standards of international law, clearing up one of the anomalies of human rights law relating to children. While the Convention defines a child as any person under 18, and accords them a variety of rights, protection from use as a soldier is denied those of 15, 16 or 17 years. Presumably this is the result of wishing to keep the standards of international humanitarian law, with the age 15 provision of the Additional Protocols to the Geneva Conventions, compatible with international human rights law. For whatever reason, it is an anomaly and should be changed. The child soldiers issue is too important to be distanced from the broader international regime of child protection in this way.

Unfortunately, some developed countries have sought to block this development, normally because they wish to recruit those who will not go on to further education, as they are essential for the lower ranks of their armed forces. If these children leave school at 16, they are likely to find alternative careers if the armed forces cannot recruit them for a further two years. As a result the campaign for the Optional Protocol has not been an easy one, and a standard which appears so morally obvious is still frustratingly out of reach. It is tempting, or at least commonplace, to focus on children as victims in time of conflict and there is certainly good reason for this. However, it is also important to realise that children are actors in conflicts, particularly when conflict is seen in the longer term, with visible cycles of violence, where the failure to bury yesterday's war has provided fertile ground for today's, and today's war is conducted without thought for the seeming inevitability of tomorrow's.

Link to the future
Children are involved in conflict in the longer term beyond picking up a gun – or having one thrust into their hands. Children are an essential

arı
atır
tutur

, Anar, arı, arıl
Anar oturur. Turan ora atılır.
Arılar aralanır.

tut

tutur

asta

usta

stol

stul

İsa

Nisa

Aslan

Soltan

Turan, o narı at o

an narı atır.

ralə,

ə onu

arı arılar atı

ları otarır.

link in the chain of violence which is so apparent in so many conflicts. Children can carry ethnic hatred between generations.

After or even during the conflict there are two imperatives relating to children. First, they must not be put in a position where they are taught to hate, either directly or indirectly as a result of their circumstances. Secondly, all efforts to restore normality and peace to war-affected communities must start with the situation of children. As an example, the children of the West Bank and Gaza have grown up in particularly difficult circumstances. They have seen their education damaged. They have seen school friends stopped from getting to hospital at checkpoints. They may have had to leave school to work to help support their family, because their fathers have been made unemployed by the virtual economic blockade they live under. And they may have seen people shot, or fired upon, or relatives taken for questioning and tortured.

It is difficult to see how any peace process can be effective when there has been a failure to help children make a positive contribution to peace. Decent schools with decent books might have at least as much value as internationally brokered peace-deals. It is not a case of one or the other. It needs to be recognised that children can make a positive or negative contribution to the longer-term process of post-conflict reconstruction. Children have to be put at the heart of peace building.

In El Salvador, a small organisation called *Pro Busqueda* tries to locate children who were abducted during the war. Abduction of children as a method of warfare is surprisingly common: the children are often unharmed and sometimes brought up as if they were the abductors' own. This pattern, apparently a way of asserting dominance over your enemy, is seen in many conflicts from El Salvador to Kurdistan. *Pro Busqueda*, set up and run by a Jesuit priest, tries to trace these children for their families. Some have been adopted in other countries, others are still in El Salvador. This is not to get the children back: the war is long past, and many of them are grown up and may not remember their real families. But the families, to 'draw a line' under that part of their history, need to know what happened to their children. In many ways this sums up the importance of a community's children in the process of peace building.

This idea of drawing a line under a conflict, whether through truth commissions or tribunals, is a central one. Each unresolved issue is another argument for taking up arms again. In these situations no issues are ever more central or more essential for those being asked to forgive than those concerning their children.

There is a further reason to concentrate on children in efforts for peace. All conflicts require at least two parties to be willing to fight and kill each other. Normally their leaders persuade their people to demonise the enemy. Once a conflict has reached that stage it is usually clear that peaceful solutions to the situation will be hard to find.

However, it is seldom the case that people hold that same attitude about children. Even in the bitterest conflicts, people tend to have less enthusiasm for harming their enemy's children than they do for harming adults. Where the gap between warring parties seems unbridgeable, sometimes an agreement can be secured that children should be left out of the conflict, should be allowed, in Graça Machel's words, 'zones of peace'. It is no coincidence that when Operation Lifeline Sudan managed to negotiate a set of humanitarian principles with the Sudan People's Liberation Army, the only human rights instrument they achieved agreement on was the Convention. Similarly, it is no coincidence that the Liberation Tigers of Tamil Eelam in northern Sri Lanka has voluntarily declared itself bound by the Convention. There are other examples. So, it may sometimes be possible to try to build a humanitarian space around children in armed conflict with and through the consent of warring parties. This has not been tried often enough, and should be a priority for those seeking to modify the conduct of future conflicts.

Bullets and bombs do not discriminate, but there are enough examples of how wars can be conducted so as to attempt at least to minimise the harm to children. Conflicts can be momentarily halted for one or two 'days of tranquillity' as they have been called, to allow for vaccination programmes. Areas where children are known to play can be left deliberately free of anti-personnel mines. School buildings can be avoided when shelling is carried out – modern artillery is accurate enough to permit this. Children can be kept out of armed forces. All of these examples show how it may be possible to minimise the effects of armed conflict on children if the will is there. There will never be any such thing as a child-friendly war, but it may be possible to try to make wars slightly less child-unfriendly.

The way the world treats its children is an index of our collective humanity. It is vital that all possible efforts be made at international and domestic level both to protect children and to allow them to become positive actors in the promotion of peace. The harm that is done to children in armed conflict violates their most fundamental human rights and as such implies a responsibility in us all to do everything we can to address this. Wars may and probably will continue for the foreseeable future. In these wars, every right of the child will continue to be violated. The only possible and proper response is to make every effort to discourage the involvement of children in the wars of adults.

Street children Sabina, 9, and her sister Naifa, 4, wait in a police cell. Bombay 1994.

Conclusion

Keep children out of conflict

The catalogue of terrors in this book is vivid testimony to the war on childhood around the world. Millions of children have died; millions more will carry lifelong physical and mental scars. The devastation to individuals, their families and their communities will last beyond childhood.

The struggle to promote children's human rights goes hand in hand with the struggle to protect children in armed conflict. Children cannot enjoy their rights as children if they can become the targets of war at any time. The scale of the problem can bring a sense of powerlessness over problems which leave you numb with the sheer weight of the casualties. The involvement of children in armed conflict is a massive problem – and it is one of the great world scandals. As we reach the end of the century, the challenge now is to demonstrate the ways children can be kept out of conflict and given protection.

As this book has tried to show, children need protection in three key areas: they need protection from participation in armed conflicts; they need protection from tactics which target civilian children in armed conflicts; and they need protection when they flee conflicts and seek refuge and asylum in different countries.

Stopping child soldiers is an obvious starting point. Children are best protected from armed conflict by keeping them out of armed conflict in the first place. This means stopping their recruitment into military forces before the age of 18. This is currently one of the biggest weaknesses in the UN Convention on the Rights of the Child, as it sets 15 as the minimum age of recruitment. This limit has failed to give children adequate protection.

The 15-year age limit on child soldiers is inconsistent with the rest of the Convention. The Convention recognises various rights and grants protection to children aged 15, 16 and 17 – unless they are recruited into the armed forces. This exemption drives a coach and horses through the Convention's principal objectives: the protection of all children. Raising the limit to 18 would ensure *all* children are entitled to all the rights in the Convention, all the time.

At a practical level, the 15-year age limit has not stopped younger children from being recruited and conscripted into armed forces. In societies where official age records may be incomplete, it is often easy for a 12- or 13-year-old to pass for 15. It would, however, be another matter altogether for a 12- or 13-year-old to pass for 18. With some 300,000 children currently participating in ongoing armed conflicts, practical measures are needed.

Amnesty International has joined a coalition of non-governmental organisations to press for a new international agreement to raise the minimum level of recruitment and participation of children in armed forces to 18-years.[176] This agreement – called the Draft Optional Protocol to the UN Convention on the Rights of the Child – is being negotiated by various governments (*see Chapter 5*). It is opposed by several powerful, developed countries, like the USA. The UK's Ministry of Defence also opposes this move: currently recruitment into the British armed forces is allowed at age 16 years.

Alongside the campaign for the Draft Optional Protocol, Amnesty International believes a new convention to the International Labour Organisation (ILO) should prohibit child soldiers. The ILO is a branch of the United Nations responsible for standards at work and industry. The ILO is due to consider a new convention which will prohibit the most hazardous and exploitative forms of child labour. Amnesty International believes there cannot be many more obvious forms of hazardous work than giving children guns and ordering them to try to kill an enemy. If we are to prohibit any hazardous work for children, it must be fighting in adult wars.

These two practical proposals could be agreed and established with a modicum of political support, especially from key governments. But it will require public pressure to persuade the more influential governments to take a lead and end the use of child soldiers.

Stopping children from become the victims of armed conflict will take longer to achieve. It will require drastic changes to military

---

[176] The International Coalition to Stop the Use of Child Soldiers includes among its members Amnesty International, Human Rights Watch, the International Save the Children Alliance, International Federation Terre des Hommes, the Jesuit Refugee Service and the Quaker UN Office (Geneva).

tactics, which have made attacks on civilians a 'normal' feature of war. We are now conditioned to expect massive civilian casualties in any conflict. The prospects for changing this 'normality' may appear slight, given the scale of the task. But it is possible to foresee change. The targeting of children in wars is not accidental. International humanitarian standards have established basic rules of war.[177] Children are caught up in armed conflicts because someone chooses to allow them to be caught up in them. Their right to protection from war is consciously ignored.

The positive side to this story is that armies are disciplined structures: Soldiers are trained to obey orders which may even jeopardise their lives. Military orders *can* be issued to prohibit attacks on children. Military discipline can ensure that transgressors are punished. Among the carnage of war in the 20th century are examples where civilian populations and their core infrastructure, like schools, have not been targeted. Rape is not an automatic assault by soldiers against their captives. It can be prohibited, prosecuted and punished.

A parallel has to be drawn with the use of chemical and biological weapons and the changing response of military leaders to the campaign against anti-personnel weapons. The public horror at the sufferings experienced by troops under gas attack in the trenches in World War One led to the 1925 Geneva Protocol, banning the use of poison gases and germ warfare. While individual governments have experimented with such weapons, the ban on using such weapons has been almost universally maintained.[178] Any military advantage gained by such weapons would be wiped out by the scale of public abhorrence. Such weapons are publicly unacceptable. World opinion is implacably opposed to their use.

The campaign to ban anti-personnel mines faced the problem that, as they had developed in sophistication and scale of deployment, anti-personnel mines had become part of the military equation. They were built in to military strategies; their manufacture and export were worth millions of pounds every year. But military arguments – for using anti-personnel mines in certain cases, and keeping them in their armoury

---

[177] See "Basic rules of the Geneva Conventions and their Additional Protocols, Chapter IV." International Committee of Red Cross & Red Crescent. www\icrc.org\
[178] See "Technology of Killing", Eric Prokosch, Zed Books, 1995, pp168-170. The notable exception in recent years to the avoidance of poison and nerve gas weapons is Iraq in the 1980s, which used chemical weapons against Iranian troops and then against Kurdish settlements in northern Iraq.

'just in case' – were swept aside. What mattered was the cruelty of these weapons and their negative effect on societies. In the face of a massive public and political campaign, military leaders previously opposed to the ban have come to accept, and in some cases even support it.

Public opposition also helped break another logjam over crimes against humanity committed during the wars in the former Yugoslavia. Public pressure forced the international community to create an *ad hoc* war crimes tribunal, first for the former Yugoslavia, then for Rwanda. The international community was soon considering the often-delayed proposal to create a permanent international court. Such a court was first proposed and debated in the aftermath of World War Two, but was an early casualty of the Cold War. In July 1998, 120 countries voted to adopt a statute to create an International Criminal Court in which the world's war criminals can be prosecuted. The new Court's primary strength will be its deterrent effect against future offences.

Public pressure can also ensure that governments provide adequate protection to children who escape armed conflict. As wars have erupted around the world over the past 20 years, the numbers of refugees have more than doubled. More people have escaped these conflicts and sought sanctuary in other countries. Millions of children have been displaced from their homes and live in temporary camps. A handful manage to escape and seek sanctuary in developed nations. But those children who seek the protection of the wealthier nations are often treated like criminals. Children as young as 12 have been detained in the UK when they have claimed asylum. The UK's reservation to the UN Convention of the Rights of the Child gives it a 'get out' clause. The Convention's protection is denied to any child seeking asylum in the UK. This cynical manoeuvre undermines a major international human rights treaty.

On the threshold of a new era for human rights, the struggle to end the impunity of war criminals will be matched by a growing awareness of children's human rights. Public opposition will be vital to stop child soldiers and to ensure that children are not targeted in wars of the future. The cruelty of involving children in armed conflicts must be exposed and condemned universally.

Killing, maiming and torturing children in pursuit of military objectives is as unacceptable as using chemical weapons. The indifference of political and military leaders towards the crimes committed at their behest cannot go unchallenged. Indiscriminate attacks – with no attempt to distinguish between soldiers and children

offering financial assistance in case of need; (c) Make higher education accessible to all on the basis of capacity by every appropriate means; (d) Make educational and vocational information and guidance available and accessible to all children; (e) Take measures to encourage regular attendance at schools and the reduction of drop-out rates.

2. States Parties shall take all appropriate measures to ensure that school discipline is administered in a manner consistent with the child's human dignity and in conformity with the present Convention.

3. States Parties shall promote and encourage international co-operation in matters relating to education, in particular with a view to contributing to the elimination of ignorance and illiteracy throughout the world and facilitating access to scientific and technical knowledge and modern teaching methods. In this regard, particular account shall be taken of the needs of developing countries.

Article 29

1. States Parties agree that the education of the child shall be directed to: (a) The development of the child's personality, talents and mental and physical abilities to their fullest potential; (b) The development of respect for human rights and fundamental freedoms, and for the principles enshrined in the Charter of the United Nations; (c) The development of respect for the child's parents, his or her own cultural identity, language and values, for the national values of the country in which the child is living, the country from which he or she may originate, and for civilizations different from his or her own; (d) The preparation of the child for responsible life in a free society, in the spirit of understanding, peace, tolerance, equality of sexes, and friendship among all peoples, ethnic, national and religious groups and persons of indigenous origin; (e) The development of respect for the natural environment.

2. No part of the present article or article 28 shall be construed so as to interfere with the liberty of individuals and bodies to establish and direct educational institutions, subject always to the observance of the principles set forth in paragraph 1 of the present article and to the requirements that the education given in such institutions shall conform to such minimum standards as may be laid down by the State.

Article 30

In those States in which ethnic, religious or linguistic minorities or persons of indigenous origin exist, a child belonging to such a minority or who is indigenous shall not be denied the right, in community with other members of his or her group, to enjoy his or her own culture, to profess and practise his or her own religion, or to use his or her own language.

Article 31

1. States Parties recognize the right of the child to rest and leisure, to engage in play and recreational activities appropriate to the age of the child and to participate freely in cultural life and the arts.

2. States Parties shall respect and promote the right of the child to participate fully in cultural and artistic life and shall encourage the provision of appropriate and equal opportunities for cultural, artistic, recreational and leisure activity.

Article 32

1. States Parties recognize the right of the child to be protected from economic exploitation and from performing any work that is likely to be hazardous or to interfere with the child's education, or to be harmful to the child's health or physical, mental, spiritual, moral or social development.

2. States Parties shall take legislative, administrative, social and educational measures to ensure the implementation of the present article. To this end, and having regard to the relevant provisions of other international instruments, States Parties shall in particular: (a) Provide for a minimum age or minimum ages for admission to employment; (b) Provide for appropriate regulation of the hours and conditions of employment; (c) Provide for appropriate penalties or other sanctions to ensure the effective enforcement of the present article.

Article 33

States Parties shall take all appropriate measures, including legislative, administrative, social and educational measures, to protect children from the illicit use of narcotic drugs and psychotropic substances as defined in the relevant international treaties, and to prevent the use of children in the illicit production and trafficking of such substances.

Article 34

States Parties undertake to protect the child from all forms of sexual exploitation and sexual abuse. For these purposes, States Parties shall in particular take all appropriate national, bilateral and multilateral measures to prevent: (a) The inducement or coercion of a child to engage in any unlawful sexual activity; (b) The exploitative use of children in prostitution or other unlawful sexual practices; (c) The exploitative use of children in pornographic performances and materials.

Article 35

States Parties shall take all appropriate national, bilateral and multilateral measures to prevent the abduction of, the sale of or traffic in children for any purpose or in any form.

Article 36

States Parties shall protect the child against all other forms of exploitation prejudicial to any aspects of the child's welfare.

Article 37

States Parties shall ensure that: (a) No child shall be subjected to torture or other cruel, inhuman or degrading treatment or punishment. Neither capital punishment nor life imprisonment without possibility of release shall be imposed for offenses committed by persons below eighteen years of age; (b) No child shall be deprived of his or her liberty unlawfully or arbitrarily. The arrest, detention or imprisonment of a child shall be in conformity with the law and shall be used only as a measure of last resort and for the shortest appropriate period of time; (c) Every child deprived of liberty shall be treated with humanity and respect for the inherent dignity of the human person, and in a manner which takes into account the needs of persons of his or her age. In particular, every child deprived of liberty shall be separated from adults unless it is considered in the child's best interest not to do so and shall have the right to maintain contact with his or her family through correspondence and visits, save in exceptional circumstances; (d) Every child deprived of his or her liberty shall have the right to prompt access to legal and other appropriate assistance, as well as the right to challenge the legality of the deprivation of his or her liberty before a court or other competent, independent and impartial authority, and to a prompt decision on any such action.

Article 38

1. States Parties undertake to respect and to ensure respect for rules of international humanitarian law applicable to them in armed conflicts which are relevant to the child.
2. States Parties shall take all feasible measures to ensure that persons who have not attained the age of fifteen years do not take a direct part in hostilities.
3. States Parties shall refrain from recruiting any person who has not attained the age of fifteen years into their armed forces. In recruiting among those persons who have attained the age of fifteen years but who have not attained the age of eighteen years, States Parties shall endeavour to give priority to those who are oldest.
4. In accordance with their obligations under international humanitarian law to protect the civilian population in armed conflicts, States Parties shall take all feasible measures to ensure protection and care of children who are affected by an armed conflict.

Article 39

States Parties shall take all appropriate measures to promote physical and psychological recovery and social reintegration of a child victim of: any form of neglect, exploitation, or abuse; torture or any other form of cruel, inhuman or degrading treatment or punishment; or armed conflicts. Such recovery and reintegration shall take place in an environment which fosters the health, self-respect and dignity of the child.

Article 40

1. States Parties recognize the right of every child alleged as, accused of, or recognized as having infringed the penal law to be treated in a manner consistent with the promotion of the child's sense of dignity and worth, which reinforces the child's respect for the human rights and fundamental freedoms of others and which takes into account the child's age and the desirability of promoting the child's reintegration and the child's assuming a constructive role in society.

2. To this end, and having regard to the relevant provisions of international instruments, States Parties shall, in particular, ensure that: (a) No child shall be alleged as, be accused of, or recognized as having infringed the penal law by reason of acts or omissions that were not prohibited by national or international law at the time they were committed; (b) Every child alleged as or accused of having infringed the penal law has a least the following guarantees: (i) To be presumed innocent until proven guilty according to law;(ii) To be informed promptly and directly of the charges against him or her, and, if appropriate, through his or her parents or legal guardians, and to have legal or other appropriate assistance in the preparation and presentation of his or her defence;(iii) To have the matter determined without delay by a competent, independent and impartial authority or judicial body in a fair hearing according to law, in the presence of legal or other appropriate assistance and, unless it is considered not to be in the best interest of the child, in particular, taking into account his or her age or situation, his or her parents or legal guardians; (iv) Not to be compelled to give testimony or to confess guilt; to examine or have examined adverse witnesses and to obtain the participation and examination of witnesses on his or her behalf under conditions of equality; (v) If considered to have infringed the penal law, to have this decision and any measures imposed in consequence thereof reviewed by a higher competent, independent and impartial authority or judicial body according to law; (vi) To have the free assistance of an interpreter if the child cannot understand or speak the language used; (vii) To have his or her privacy fully respected at all stages of the proceedings.

3. States Parties shall seek to promote the establishment of laws, procedures, authorities and institutions specifically applicable to children alleged as, accused of, or recognized as having infringed the penal law, and, in particular: (a) The establishment of a minimum age below which children shall be presumed not to have the capacity to infringe the penal law; (b) Whenever appropriate and desirable,

measures for dealing with such children without resorting to judicial proceedings, providing that human rights and legal safeguards are fully respected.

4. A variety of dispositions, such as care, guidance and supervision orders; counselling; probation; foster care; education and vocational training programmes and other alternatives to institutional care shall be available to ensure that children are dealt with in a manner appropriate to their well-being and proportionate both to their circumstances and the offence.

Article 41

Nothing in the present Convention shall affect any provisions which are more conducive to the realization of the rights of the child and which may be contained in: (a) The law of a State Party; or (b) International law in force for that State.

Articles 42 to 54 are of an administrative nature and therefore have not been reproduced in this volume.

World Council of Churches, December 1998 Statement on Child Soldiers

Hundreds of thousands of children under the age of eighteen, girls as well as boys, are enrolled today in national or irregular armed forces around the world. More than 300,000 children are currently engaged in armed conflicts. Many have been lawfully recruited, others have been kidnaped or otherwise coerced, the overwhelming majority of child soldiers come from marginalized and excluded sectors of society.

The involvement of children in armed conflicts violates fundamental humanitarian principles, exposes them to the risk of death and injury, threatens their physical, mental, emotional and spiritual well-being, and draws them into a culture of violence.

The Eighth Assembly of the World Council of Churches meeting in Harare, Zimbabwe 3-14 December 1998:

1. Recalls the affirmation of the First Assembly that war is contrary to the will of God;
2. Renews its commitment to seek the delegitimization of war and violence and to strive to overcome the spirit, logic and practice of war;
3. Restates its opposition to any policy or authority which violates the rights of the younger generation, abuses or exploits them;
4. Condemns any use of children in warfare;
5. Calls upon its member churches to:
   call for an immediate moratorium on the recruitment and participation of children as soldiers and the demobilization of existing child soldiers;
   assist those engaged in the rehabilitation, social reintegration and reconciliation; of former child soldiers, taking particular account of the needs of former girl soldiers;
   work to prevent the compulsory or voluntary recruitment or re-recruitment of children as soldiers in national armies or irregular armed forces or groups;
   promote the establishment of international standards to this effect, in particular the adoption of an optional protocol to the Convention on the Rights of the Child raising the minimum age from 15 to 18 years for all forms of recruitment and participation in hostilities;
   urge their national governments to adopt and apply such standards in their own national legislation.
6. Calls especially upon member churches in Africa to advocate for the prompt ratification by their governments of the African Charter on the Rights and Welfare of the Child which prohibits the recruitment to armed forces and participation in hostilities of children under 18 years.

Amnesty International reports

Sierra Leone: 1998 - a year of atrocities against civilians. AI Index AFR 51/22/98. November 1998. This report deals extensively with the plight of children in the internal armed conflict in Sierra Leone. It provides up-to-date information on the situation of children in Sierra Leone, including commitments this year by the government and the civilian militia supporting the government, the Civil Defence Forces (CDF), not to recruit children under 18 years, the continuing abduction and forcible recruitment of children by rebel forces of the Armed Forces Revolutionary Council (AFRC) and the Revolutionary United Front (RUF), and efforts by the international community to meet the needs of children in Sierra Leone.

'Old enough to kill but too young to vote'. Draft optional protocol to the Convention on the Rights of the Child on the involvement of children in armed conflicts. AI Index: IOR 51/1/98. January 1998.

Children in South Asia: Securing their rights. AI Index ASA 4/1/98. April 1998.

Uganda: 'Breaking God's commands'. The destruction of childhood by the Lord's resistance Army. AI Index AFR 59/1/97. September 1997.

Rwanda: Alarming resurgence of killings. AI Index AR 47/13/96. August 1996.

Rwanda: Mass murder by government supporters and troops in April and May 1994. AI Index AFR 47/11/94. May 1996.

Rwanda: Crying out for justice. AI Index AFR 47/5/95. April 1995.

Rwanda: Persecution of Tutsi minority and repression of government critics, 1990-1992. AI Index AFR 47/2/92. May 1992.

Rwanda: Amnesty International's concerns since the beginning of an insurgency in October 1990. AI Index AFR 47/5/91. March 1991.

The Amnesty International Mandate

Amnesty International is a worldwide voluntary movement of 1.1 million people that works to prevent some of the gravest violations by governments of people's fundamental human rights. The main focus of its campaigning is to:

- free all prisoners of conscience. These are people detained anywhere for their beliefs, or by reason of their ethnic origin, sex, colour, language, national or social origin, economic status, birth, or other status – who have not used or advocated violence;
- ensure fair and prompt trials for political prisoners;
- abolish the death penalty, torture and other cruel treatment of prisoners;
- end extra-judicial executions and 'disappearances'.

Amnesty International, also opposes abuses by opposition groups: hostage-taking, torture and killings of prisoners and other arbitrary killings.

Amnesty International is impartial. It is independent of any government, political persuasion or religious creed. It does not support or oppose any government or political system, nor does it support or oppose views of the victims whose rights it seeks to protect. It is concerned solely with the protection of the human rights involved in each case, regardless of the ideology of the government, opposition forces or the beliefs of the individual. Amnesty International is financed by sub-scriptions and donations from its world-wide membership. No funds are sought or accepted from governments.

Amnesty International, recognising that human rights are indivisible and inter-dependent, works to promote all the human rights enshrined in the Universal Declaration of Human Rights and other international standards, through its human rights education programmes and campaigning for ratification of human rights treaties.

Children's Human Rights Network

Amnesty International also has a Children's Human Rights Network, which members can join, which works to promote children's rights and campaign against child rights violations.

Children's Rights Campaign

In 1999, Amnesty International UK's campaign on children's rights marks the 10th anniversary of the UN Convention on the Rights of the Child. It highlights children in armed conflict, street children and children in detention. Amnesty International has called for the UK Government to support moves to ban the use of child soldiers, raising the minimum age of recruitment to 18, and pressing for an Optional Protocol to the Convention on the Rights of the Child (*see page 99*). And it has pressed for the government to ensure adequate protection for children fleeing violations when they seek asylum in the UK.

Children's Rights CD-Rom

Just Right!, an inter-active CD-rom for children (Key stages 3 and 4) is a highly inter-active way to get children to appreciate the importance of the UN Convention on the Rights of the Child, and different aspects of children's rights. It comes with teacher's notes.

Available from February, price £10. To order, contact Amnesty International on tel: 01788 545 553 (for credit cards), or at Amnesty International, Aventine Way, Glebe Farm Industrial Estate, Rugby, Warks CV21 1RH (cheques). Quote Product Code CC005.

For more information and details of membership contact:

Amnesty International United Kingdom
99-119 Rosebery Avenue, London, EC1R 4RE
Tel: 0171-814 6200   Fax: 0171-833 1510
Website: http://www.amnesty.org.uk/